THE MIEGUNYAH PRESS

THIS IS NUMBER ONE HUNDRED AND THIRTEEN IN THE

SECOND NUMBERED SERIES OF THE

MIEGUNYAH VOLUMES

MADE POSSIBLE BY THE

MIEGUNYAH FUND

ESTABLISHED BY BEQUESTS

UNDER THE WILLS OF

SIR RUSSELL AND LADY GRIMWADE.

'MIEGUNYAH' WAS THE HOME OF

MAB AND RUSSELL GRIMWADE

FROM 1911 TO 1955.

Gardens of Eden

Written and photographed by

HOLLY KERR FORSYTH

Among the World's Most Beautiful Gardens

THE MIEGUNYAH PRESS

ACKNOWLEDGEMENTS

There are so many people who have contributed to this book and whose generosity and hard work have made its publication possible. I am most grateful to all the owners who have allowed me to write about and photograph their gardens. My thanks go, too, to the curators and head gardeners who made time to show me their gardens, answer countless questions and provide details of plant species and varieties.

Heartfelt gratitude goes to garden owners, friends and colleagues who provided warm and generous hospitality, which allowed me to photograph from dawn. And to those who spurred me on to seek out the perfect photograph—like John Hawkins, who admonished, 'We must climb!', when I suggested we drive to the top of Tasmania's glorious Western Tiers to capture the *genius loci* or sense of place. Thus began a terrifying, but ultimately exhilarating, experience. To friends like Ivan Saltmarsh, for his encouragement, good company and expert advice on good photo angles—when my focus had started to wander towards hot, strong coffee. And to my friend Sally Williams, who chaperoned me around the glorious gardens of the east coast of the United States. My thanks, again, to Sue Home, who accompanied me on several trips.

Many organisations also provided entrée to and information on the marvellous gardens in this book. My thanks to the Japan Imperial Household for providing access to the extraordinary Kyoto gardens, and to the Australian Embassy in Tokyo. The great Japanese landscaper Shiro Nakane, and his colleague in Australia, Ken Lamb, generously provided advice and access to so many special Japanese gardens. My friends in Japan, Taeko and John Crawley and Akinori Muro, also assisted me with access to gardens and permissions to photograph.

In Italy, Tourism Vicenza, Tourism Stressa and Tourism Como provided information and wonderful hospitality; the Irish Tourist Board opened my eyes to the wonderful gardens in its country. And among the greatest gardens in the United Kingdom are those owned by the National Trust. Likewise, Virginia Tourism, Tourism Singapore, Tourism New Zealand and Hamish Saxton at Tourism Dunedin provided streamlined access to their great gardens and made the job of photographing and interviewing so much easier.

The botanist Dr Peter Valder kindly helped me identify species, and Vica Bayley of the Wilderness Society, Tasmania, assisted me in sorting through the somewhat difficult maze that is forest politics in that state.

I am again fortunate to have the support of Louise Adler, Chief Executive at Melbourne University Publishing; I am also indebted to Tracy O'Shaughnessy, for her vision and insight, and Eugenie Baulch and the entire team at MUP. My thanks, too, to editor Judy Brookes, to Dave Bishop for his file management, and to Hamish Freeman for his wonderful design.

And, as always, my greatest accolades and gratitude go to my husband, Ross, my daughters, Olivia and Camilla, and my sons, Angus and Tom, for their patience and unstinting, loving support.

And the Lord God formed man of the dust of the ground,
and breathed ... the breath of life;
and man became a living soul.
And the Lord God planted a garden eastward in Eden ...

GENESIS 2:7–8

INTRODUCTION

We all have our own idea of paradise. For some of us, paradise is our own garden; for others, it is someone else's. And for yet others, it is a pristine wilderness, untouched by humankind. Perhaps the best gardens are those that speak eloquently of the natural landscape in which they are located. A garden, however, is the imposition of human intent upon nature, no matter how light the hand with which it is made.

The Scottish John Claudius Loudon (1783–1843), the most prolific garden writer of the nineteenth century, believed that human behaviour is influenced by environment: imagine mean streets softened by plantings of shade-giving trees, and think of community gardens, in which social interaction and the sense of sharing and co-operation are as important as the plants coaxed from the soil. Think of sensory gardens of fragrant herbs, designed for the physically or visually impaired, or of pots of cascading ivy-leaved geraniums that brighten the smallest balcony after a dreary winter. There is surely nothing that will provide a greater sense of exhilaration and inspiration than a thing of natural beauty. And it is clear from the gardens in this book, which have been created over the centuries, that the pursuit of this beauty—perhaps in its simplest and purest guise, the garden—is a universal goal.

Throughout time, changes in economic and social circumstances have found expression through the creation of gardens. We can read a culture by its gardens; judge its political landscape. Through turmoil and change, one thing has remained constant: people have gardened as a means of finding solace and comfort. In the midst of human tragedy and environmental disaster, beauty and good can be salvaged and created from the earth; such endeavour is essential for survival and sanity.

Garden-making is perhaps the greatest of all the decorative arts, revered since pre-history. The paradise garden has formed the basis of garden-making since the Persian Empire and, from there, spread east along the various silk routes to influence the Mughal gardens of India. At the same time, its influence spread west into Spain and Italy, transported by the warriors of the Crusades.

While researching and writing this book—and while travelling throughout the world, photographing the gardens, and interviewing owners, landscapers and historians—I have been struck, yet again, by the repeated evidence that the rules of good garden-making transcend geographical boundaries

Previous page: At the Manor House in the English village of Upton Grey, in Hampshire, swags of roses and clematis add structure and year-round excitement to the picking garden.

Opposite: Katsura Rikyu, Kyoto, was completed around 1649 by Imperial Prince Toshihito's son, the scholarly Prince Toshitada, in the Edo Period (1603–1867). It was designed to lead guests on a journey, often across beautiful bridges. Toshitada hosted tea ceremonies, moon viewing and boating parties, when the reflections of buildings and trees could be best appreciated. It is thought that much of the garden was inspired by literature of the Heian Period (794–1185), most particularly Shikibu Murasaki's *Tale of the Genji*, with its descriptions of idyllic gardens and reflections upon the fleeting beauty of nature. The Heian Period—when Kyoto was first known as Heian-kyo, meaning the Capital of Peace and Tranquility—was the golden age for the city, when all the arts were honoured, including garden-making.

and the cultures they constrain. From Europe to the Middle East and on to China and Japan, and then to the southern hemisphere, good gardens—consciously or not—employ a common set of principles.

While gardens are an expression of personal taste, many of us are voyeurs of other people's gardens: through visits, and through books. They allow us to dream of what might have been had we more time or greater means. No matter how grand, however, all gardens provide vignettes, ideas, which we can borrow to contribute to our own paradise.

This book is not simply a stroll through the world's greatest gardens; it is also a romp through history and an armchair ride around the globe. It is a celebration of ideals and aesthetics that are central to all cultures, important to each in the creation of its landscapes. From the legacy of the rulers of ancient Persia—modern-day Iran—to the Buddhist-inspired landscape aesthetic of China and Japan, the restrained gardens of Italy, the subtle hues of Provence, and the treasure-filled gardens of England, this book seeks to explain the central themes—the heart—of gardening.

The intrepid plant hunter Ernest Henry 'Chinese' Wilson (1876–1930) summed it up for us when he wrote in *Smoke that Thunders*, 'Nature is a generous mother and with flower and leaf has decked the world in loveliness. Love of the beautiful in organic and inorganic life is the most elevating influence permeating the human family. There are no happier folk than plant lovers and none more generous than those who garden.'

We can understand that fascination and passion, no matter where we garden.

Use of people's names

It is useful to clarify the use of first names and surnames in this book. The men and women discussed throughout are referred to by their first names if their gardens are private spaces. Professional landscapers, architects, writers and artists, however, are referred to by their surnames, as is the usual journalistic style.

Use of botanical names

This book follows the latest regulations of the International Code of Nomenclature for Cultivated Plants (7th edition) published in 2002 by the International Society for Horticultural Science. As readers will know, the genus and the species of a plant are written in italics, while the names of plant cultivars are written in roman type, starting with a capital letter and enclosed by single quotation marks. For example, *Magnolia liliiflora* 'Nigra'.

The exception to this rule is the many genera of orchids, the only group of plants where hybrid names, known as grex epithets, are registered with the Royal Horticultural Society (RHS) in London. All hybrids, whether humanmade or naturally occurring, do not attract single quotes. For instance, the hybrid between the two *Coelogyne* species, *cristata* and *flaccida* is always called *Coelogyne* Unchained Melody. No single inverted commas are used as it is not a cultivar; it is a hybrid. Selected clones of this hybrid may be granted cultivar names—these differentiate related, but slightly different, plants: for instance, *Coelogyne* Unchained Melody 'Mary'. To further check on parentage of orchids, go to www.rhs.org.uk/plants/registerpages/orchid_parentage.asp

LESSONS IN
GARDEN HISTORY

The significance of garden-making has been evident since pre-history. The great paradise gardens of Persia, and their design principles, spread east and then west to underline the magnificence of rulers for hundreds of years. Garden design was one of the arts that illuminated the supremacy of the Italian Renaissance. Then, the movement instigated by the three great landscapers of eighteenth-century England—and influenced by the perfect romantic landscapes of painters Claude (1600–1682), Poussin (1594–1665) and Rosa (1615–1673)—was fuelled by the new wealth of the Industrial Revolution. The nineteenth century was marked by the more relaxed style of William Robinson, who treated nature as his muse, and by that of Gertrude Jekyll—although she, in turn, saw merit in the disciplined palette of formal European gardens. Horticulture around the world has been inspired by China's botanical riches, and lives and fortunes were risked as the world grew closer—and the plant hunters of the West competed for the botanical treasures of the East.

THE
Paradise Gardens
OF
Iran

The Great King ... in all the districts he resides in and visits ... takes care that there are 'paradises' ... full of all the good and beautiful things that the soil will produce.

GREEK HISTORIAN, SOLDIER AND WRITER XENOPHON (C. 431–352 BC)
ON CYRUS THE GREAT, WHO RULED THE PERSIAN EMPIRE FROM 559–539 BC,
AND CREATED THE GREATEST STATE OF ITS DAY

They have been making gardens in Iran—ancient Persia—since pre-history, when Cyrus, the founder of the Achaemenid dynasty (550–330 BC), created his capital at Pasargadae, along with the earliest garden for which records and relics remain.

Gardens form an integral part of Iranian culture, depicted in decorative arts and represented in literature over many thousands of years. From the earliest times, Persian gardens were created as the earthly representations, or reflections, of paradise, an idea that became central to many cultures and religions throughout later centuries. Water, earth and trees are considered sacred in pre-Islamic and Islamic culture; beauty, reflecting light, deflects evil.

The word *paradise* is derived from the Persian word *pairidaeza*, a royal hunting park or enclosure containing fruit trees. It conjures up images of an idealised and ordered world, a benign and secure environment, a place of abundance and safety, where streams of milk and honey flow constantly. Paradise, with its four rivers, is central to Judeo-Christian and Islamic traditions—and is revealed in both the Bible and the Qur'an. At

Opposite: The Bagh-e Shah-zadeh, or Prince's Garden, was constructed in the early 1880s in the desert at Mahan, near Kerman, southern Iran. A series of terraces creates cascades at intervals in the central, rectangular waterway, which, set with fountains and edged with wide flowerbeds, leads from the entrance gate to the governor's house.

Above: The road to Yaszd descends the mountain pass through the Zagros Mountains, from ancient times the chief north–south route through Iran. The giant fennel (*Ferula assa-foetida*) blooms in April. **Opposite, top:** The Chehel Sotun Palace, in Isfahan—the capital of Persia under the Safavid Period (1501–1736)—was built in 1647. In Iranian gardens the outside merges with interior spaces; here, a traditional platform affords views over the garden. **Opposite, bottom:** Kashan's Bagh-e Fin, or Fin Garden, was built some 400 years ago by Shah Abbas I and is an excellent example of the Iranian skill in harnessing water. Spring water is diverted into the garden, where it runs through a long waterway lined with turquoise tiles. Trees and water are this garden's two most important elements.

the heart of the idea of paradise, therefore, is a bountiful, ordered, enclosed space in which water is directed in four ways, emanating from, and returning to, a central source.

Iranian gardens are symmetrical, created around this idea of enclosure and privacy, a safe place reflecting God's paradise. They employ a restricted palette of flowers and trees that provide shade for rest and contemplation. Space is dissected into balanced squares and rectangles by paths and cooling waterways; uninterrupted vistas across the garden are important. To this end, the central area contains low plants and, of course, pools and rills. The main pathways that skirt the garden boundaries are usually lined with cypress, plane trees and mulberries, underplanted with Iran's national tree, the Judas tree (*Cercis siliquas-trum*), silk tree (*Albizia julibrissin*) or oleander. Citrus are important, particularly in the gardens of the southern city of Shiraz.

Water—pure, refreshing, mesmerising—is a precious component and has become central to gardens throughout history. Iranian gardens are often gently sloping, to encourage the flow of water, and terraced.

Iran's extensive underground water storage system of *qanat* (pronounced 'canart')—much of which remains in working order—has long provided essential drinking water and irrigation for crops of rape and corn and orchards of pomegranate, almonds and quince, which

flower in clouds of delicate blossom in villages and towns. The Iranian love of agriculture and verdant landscapes is evident across the country, thanks to the melting snows from its mountains and, in part, to this sophisticated system of wells, some of which reach down 200 metres. Built in the Persian period, from the sixth century BC, these chains of dome-topped pits are connected by thousands of kilometres of underground galleries. They once provided oases for travellers, who gathered around in caravanserai (roadside inns), often on the lower slopes of the mountains.

Iran is a land of extremes, from the flat, brown desert of the high central plateau—almost a moonscape—to the soaring, jagged, snow-covered mountains, which tower above on either side. Across the north of the country, from east to west, lie the Alborz Mountains and from north to south on the western side of the country, flanking the desert plateau, stretch the Zagros Mountains which, in pre-history, protected the empire from invasion from Mesopotamia. Fertile north-south valleys cut through the mountains, but the southern part of the high plateau is a salt desert.

Vividly described by eighteenth-century European travellers, Persian gardens had long enchanted kings and emperors from surrounding regions. In 1387, from his capital Samarkand—in modern Uzbekistan—the Central Asian prince and military genius Timur, or Tamerlane (c. 1335–1405), ordered the four grandest gardens in Shiraz to be copied for the city, as well as architectural treasures such as the exquisite tile-decorated, brilliantly coloured mosques, the most important symbol of Islamic culture. Timur's conquests—from the Mediterranean to India in the east and far into Russia—formed the basis for the Mughal Empire. The beautiful walled gardens of Samarkand inspired Timur's descendant Babur (1483–1530) to build similar gardens at Kabul in modern Afghanistan and at Agra in northern India.

In Islamic gardens, springtime signifies God's grace: orchards, meadows and gardens burst into life, brightening the desert that covers much of the Muslim world. In April, the Judas tree flowers cerise against a clear blue sky. Fields of golden crops, copses of poplars reaching for the heavens, and clouds of fruit and nut blossom spilling over ancient mud walls are among the abundant sights. Spring also heralds wildflowers in Iran, from endemic species of foxtail lily (*Eremurus* spp.), glinting white beneath snowy peaks, to carpets of red poppies and tiny species tulips, miraculously surviving among the rocky terrain.

> *Last night the wind from out her village blew*
> *And wandered all the garden alleys through*
> *Oh rose, tearing thy bosom's robe in two;*
> *Twas not in vain!*

EARLY FOURTEENTH-CENTURY PERSIAN MYSTIC AND POET HĀFEZ

Top, left: The new capital of Isfahan was built by Shah Abbas I (who ruled 1587–1629) after he defeated the Central Asian warlords, and reached the height of its splendour during the second half of the seventeenth century. The city's main square remains the glorious Maydan-e-shah—or Imperial, or Imam, Square—with arcades of shops, a cavernous bazaar and magnificent mosques. It is easy to see why the 8-hectare square—five times the size of Venice's St Mark's Square—has long been regarded as an unparalleled architectural marvel and helped earn Isfahan the accolade, 'Isfahan is half the world'. **Top, centre and right:** Water is central to gardens throughout Iran: here, in the gardens of the Abassi Hotel in Isfahan, once a Safavid cruciform-plan caravanserai, and renovated by the last Shah into a hotel to house international guests during his flamboyant celebrations in 1971 for the 2500th anniversary of the Persian Empire. Since ancient times Iranian caravanserai have provided shelter and protection for travellers and so became trading centres. The Char-bagh Madrasah and Mosque are seen from the gardens of the hotel. **Centre:** Bagh-e Shahzadeh, or Prince's Garden, in the desert at Mahan, southern Iran. **Bottom, left:** This pigeon tower, in the suburbs of Isfahan, stands behind the pink blossom of the Judas tree, *Cercis siliquastrum*. Pigeon towers, of sun-baked mud-brick, clay and straw, were used to produce manure for agriculture. **Bottom, centre:** The Naranjestan Garden in Shiraz was built for a leading family in 1870. The blue-tiled waterway is decorated with sparkling fountains. Roses and annuals bloom on either side and are flanked by an avenue of orange trees; this central rectangle is shaded by tall date palms. **Bottom, right:** Massive terracotta pots among flowering spring annuals in the Shiraz Museum.

Villa Lante

With this one plan Bramante dictated the basis of European garden design for more than two centuries to come.

GEORGINA MASSON, *ROME*, P. 76

The three essential elements of good gardens—water, stone and evergreen plants—acquired their greatest resonance through the gardens of the Italian Renaissance during the fifteenth and sixteenth centuries. Architects, artists, writers and garden-makers flourished under the extravagant patronage of a series of wealthy families and the popes and cardinals they produced. Extraordinary gardens, such as Raphael's Villa Madama and Lippi's Villa Medici (both created for the Medici family in the sixteenth century) and Donato Bramante's extravagant arrangement for the Vatican's Cortile del Belvedere in Rome, demonstrated a perfect marriage of all the arts—design, architecture, stonemasonry and sculpture, and plantsmanship.

Even after garden-making became influenced by the desire to recreate nature in the landscaped parkland, and later, when exploration into a new world resulted in a fascination with rare and exotic plants, these elements remained central to the work of designers, from André Le Nôtre (1613–1700) to English plantswoman Gertrude Jekyll (1843–1932), her disciple American Beatrix Jones Farrand (1872–1959) and Australia's Edna Walling (1895–1973).

Opposite, left: The Villa Lante's steeply sloping site is terraced, each level restrained by stone balustrades. Here, the dining terrace was the setting for lavish entertainment; guests were often at the centre of flamboyant jokes, when complicated fountains would erupt in the midst of banquets. *Left:* The Fountain of the Flood.

Above: Villa Lante's richly patterned Lake Parterre, laid out on the lowest level of the garden, comprises four pools of water surrounded by twelve gardens of box and yew, encasing various allegorical motifs and punctuated by tubs of citrus. **Opposite:** The water chain, which cascades down a central staircase through several levels, is decorated with *gambero*, or crayfish—the Gambara family coat of arms—and is edged by closely clipped box hedges.

This restrained palette—along with the key architectural treatment of a central main axis leading through a series of terraces—is perfectly demonstrated by Villa Lante at Bagnaia, a small thirteenth-century village an hour north of Rome, known since Roman times for its mineral water. Villa Lante was created for Cardinal Gambara, a member of the powerful Farnese family, by the most important artist and garden architect of the sixteenth century, Giacomo Barrozi da Vignola (1507–1573). Commissioned in 1566, the year Gambara was made Bishop of Viterbo, the cardinal's country estate was designed for feasts, performances and entertaining.

Considered the greatest and most perfect example of High Renaissance garden art and architecture, Villa Lante is designed as a series of expansive, shaded terraces connected by complicated staircases, balustrades, cascades, rills, fountains and pools, which form the main focus of the garden. While smaller than some gardens, its symmetry and allegorical references are rivalled only by the spectacular Villa d'Este in the hills to the east of Rome, which was designed by Pirro Ligorio (1513–1583) for Ippolito II, Cardinal of Ferrara and Governor of Tivoli from 1550.

Water is crucial to the design of the gardens at Villa Lante—as, indeed, it is in all the great Italian gardens, both ancient and modern. The beautiful stepped water chain, decorated with *gambero* or crayfish—a reference to the Gambara family coat of arms—and from which several axes radiate, tumbles down a central staircase, guarded by closely clipped box hedges.

The water dances through a series of levels, pauses for a while in the Fountain of the Giants, where the massive stone river gods of the Tiber and Arno recline, before finally coming to rest in the still waters of the Lake Parterre, richly drawn in box.

On the dining terrace, water that once kept drinks cool is still channelled through a massive stone table. There, the intricate system of pipes and taps, used by the cardinal to play jokes on his guests (they erupted at unexpected times to splash the unwary in their finery) remains in working order.

To explore the gardens as Vignola intended, the visitor must climb the staircases to the summit of the garden, where water pours from a cool, fern-covered grotto—looking as if it has been formed naturally by moving water over centuries. This source—the Fountain of the Flood, designed by Vignola as a symbol of life and originating in the springs of Monte Sant'Angelo—provides the water for the entire garden. From the top terrace, which is guarded by two massive plane trees, each with a trunk some 3 metres in circumference, the view across the garden unfolds, as its creator intended, symbolising the journey from birth to death.

Opposite: Water dances through a series of terraces, pauses in the Fountain of the Giants—where the massive stone river gods of the Tiber and the Arno recline—before finally settling in Villa Lante's complicated, detailed Lake Parterre. ***Above, left***: The villa, or *casino*, is divided into two, to allow for the arrangement of the axial cascades of water and stone down the terraced hillside. The young Cardinal Gambara had only built one section, however, before he suspended work after being chastised by Pope Gregory XIII for his extravagance. ***Above, centre***: The garden's water originates in the springs of Monte Sant'Angelo, above the Villa Lante; it flows through the grotto at the upper-most level before cascading down the steeply sloping site. ***Above, right***: The Temple to the Muses, with the Gambara family emblem carved into the façade, is shaded by ancient oaks.

Harewood House

You see, sweet maid, we marry
A gentler scion to the wildest stock,
And make conceive a bark of baser kind
By bud of nobler race: this is an art
Which does mend nature, change it rather, but
The art itself is nature.

WILLIAM SHAKESPEARE, *THE WINTER'S TALE*, ACT 4, SCENE 4, LINES 92–7

We have seen that the gardens of the Italian Renaissance demonstrated humankind's reflection upon our place in the universe and our relationship with nature. The French gardens that followed during the seventeenth century strived to demonstrate superiority over, and manipulation of, nature, while from the eighteenth century English gardens sought to eulogise nature by recreating it.

Eschewing the easy ride to those glorious gardens in the south of England and venturing further afield to the north of the country, the adventurous spirit will be rewarded with gardens on a completely different scale. Many grand estates created or enlarged at the time of the Industrial Revolution in the late eighteenth and early nineteenth centuries, particularly in and around Yorkshire, continue to flourish today.

Many grounds designed by the famous trio of eighteenth-century landscape architects—William Kent, Lancelot 'Capability' Brown or Humphry Repton (*see* overleaf)—with the help of such preservation societies as English Heritage, are still magnificent. While on a scale that most of us will only experience as a guest, they provide lessons in garden design, as

Opposite: The terrace at Harewood House is dominated by a parterre of box and yew, in spring filled with tulips: here, *T.* 'Black Swan'.

ENGLISH GARDEN DESIGN

In his widely read treatise *The History of Modern Taste in Gardening,* the politician Horace Walpole wrote that William Kent, the first of the triumvirate of eighteenth-century English landscapers, 'Leapt the fence and saw that all England is a garden.' It was published in 1780 and is still quoted by writers and cultural geographers as central to the English psyche.

The work of these famous landscape designers—William Kent (1685–1748), Lancelot 'Capability' Brown (1716–1783) and Humphry Repton (1752–1818)—remains central to the style, spirit and psychology of English gardening. Their work swept away the formality of the previous centuries of Italian and French influence, with the clear message of man's supremacy over nature, to allow the landscape to effortlessly dominate.

William Kent—architect, decorator, gardener—is generally credited with the earliest innovations in an English landscape style. He was influenced by the aestheticist William Gilpin, who had declared that the park was 'one of the noblest appendages of a great house'. Nothing, wrote Gilpin, gave 'a mansion so much dignity'. Also influenced by the work of Andrea Palladio (*see* pages 81–5), among Kent's greatest work is Stowe,

Buckinghamshire, where his romantic wooded valley, the Elysian Fields, has become part of the vocabulary of perfection.

Lancelot 'Capability' Brown swept away the parterres and formal planting of seventeenth-century designers, damming rivers to create massive lakes, moving land masses to change the contours of the land, and planting forests. In his effort to emulate nature, Brown virtually banned all ornamentation from his work. Perhaps his forte, at important estates such as Chatsworth—the Derbyshire property of the Dukes of Devonshire (and arguably the most influential of all the great British gardens, since the royal gardeners, Wise and London laid out formal gardens for the 1st Duke in the 1690s) —was the creation of a fantastically beautiful lake.

Humphry Repton continued Brown's work, seeking to blur the boundaries between the garden and its surrounding landscape, but later reinstated more formal elements: terraces, balustrades, steps and flower borders, allowing art to dominate nature once again. In his famous 'Red Books', Repton showed clients—through the use of overlays— 'before' and 'after' depictions of their gardens. The first of his four weighty illustrated books on landscape gardening, *Sketches and Hints on Landscape Gardening*, was published in 1795.

well as vibrant lessons in garden history. Many are particularly interesting for gardeners and historians in the United States, Australia and New Zealand, as some of the earliest pastoral estates in the 'New World', created by emigrating English tenant farmers in the eighteenth and nineteenth centuries, were named after some of the grandest estates of 'home'.

Among the most beautiful in Yorkshire are the gardens of Harewood House, which was designed by John Carr of York (1723–1807) for Edwin Lascelles, Lord Harewood, and completed in 1772. Interiors are by the Scottish architect Robert Adam and rooms are furnished by Thomas Chippendale. Plans for the park and lake were submitted by 'Capability' Brown the same year and took nine years to implement; Humphry Repton worked on Harewood from 1800 to 1802.

In 1844, Sir Charles Barry (1795–1860), the architect of the houses of parliament—and a disciple of the Italian Renaissance—was commissioned by Louisa, wife of the 3rd Earl of Harewood, to enlarge the house to accommodate their thirteen children. Another storey was added to the house and the massive South Terrace, some 100 metres by 70 metres, was laid out. The terrace was grassed over in 1959 in an attempt to stem high labour costs before detailed planting was reinstated in 1994.

Today, the parterre is drawn in edging box (*Buxus sempervirens* 'Suffruticosa') with clipped pyramids of yew accentuating corners. Thousands of 'Black Swan' tulips along with thousands more annuals fill the segments: they are changed in the second week of June with summer plantings, often of geraniums.

The grand 15-hectare lake was a seminal part of Brown's ambitious design for the gardens. Brown was paid £6000 for his work at Harewood, which is described by his biographer, Dorothy Stroud, as 'one of the most delectable of landscapes'. His plantings of oak, linden, maple and rhododendron are now massive trees. Wonderful copper beech provide extraordinary autumn tones, augmented in Victorian times as a curtsy to the fashion for more colour in garden plantings.

A dell was created, beyond the lake, to house tender plants brought back from the eighteenth-century plant-hunting expeditions; and the present Lord Harewood's father, the 6th Earl, subscribed to Frank Kingdon-Ward's excursions to Burma in 1930. In the damp conditions of this section of the gardens, hostas, ferns and swaths of *Primula pulverulenta* and *P. florindae*—the latter named after Kingdon-Ward's wife, Florinda—thrive. There is also the coveted *Meconopsis betonicifolia,* with its electric blue flowers, the triumph of a Kingdon-Ward expedition to Tibet.

Each generation of the family has made changes, to stamp individual ideas upon this 60 hectares of extraordinary garden and park. Time also opens up vistas that perhaps provide an insight into the original vision of the designers: in 1962, during two days of gale-force winds, 30 000 trees were lost.

Harewood is not simply a house of treasures and a wonderful landscape describing lessons in garden history, however; the exciting planting will engage all garden-lovers.

Previous pages, left: Architect Sir Charles Barry designed the fountains placed throughout Harewood's terrace, which is intended to be viewed from the house above. The central fountain is contemporary, as the original was irreparably damaged by frost in the early 1980s. Four flights of stairs lead from an upper level to this lower terrace. At the base of each are plantings of *Acanthus spinosus*, matching the acanthus at the top of the columns of the house, and thus linking the house to the garden. *Previous pages, right:* This wonderful, expansive lake was central to 'Capability' Brown's design for the Harewood gardens. *Opposite:* The dell was created to house treasures brought back from plant-hunting expeditions, and the river and cascades feed from the lake. Water-loving plants, such as astilbes, persicarias, primulas and the giant rhubarb (*Gunnera manicata*) hug the banks.

Gravetye Manor

This art is a purely English one.

WILLIAM ROBINSON, *HOME LANDSCAPES*, P. V

It is clear that the English take their gardening seriously. They respect their garden history and revere their great garden designers. Nowhere is this demonstrated more clearly than Gravetye Manor, near the old town of East Grinstead, West Sussex. This Elizabethan house was home to the Irish gardener and writer William Robinson (1838–1935), considered by garden historians as the father of modern English horticulture.

Robinson purchased the 300-year-old manor in 1885 and gradually accumulated about 500 hectares of land around it. He lived and gardened at Gravetye until he died, well into his nineties.

William Robinson is generally credited as the creator of the natural, or wild, style of garden. There are no tight corsets of clipped box restraining contrived planting patterns at Gravetye; instead, voluptuous arrangements spill over pathways, and banks of rare shrubs cascade down hillsides as if nature has designed them. A gentle slope, covered in the wildflowers of the region, leads down to a vast lake and on to the woodland, now managed by the Forestry Commission.

Today Gravetye Manor is a grand country house hotel and is the only remaining Robinsonian garden in England. The property was lovingly and faithfully restored over half a century by Peter Herbert, who retired a few years ago in favour of a buy-out by two key staff: general manager

Opposite: The north lawn at Gravetye Manor, with its ancient sundial, overlooks the lakes and extensive woodlands. The light is particularly beautiful here, late on a summer afternoon; it is where the gardener and writer William Robinson often sat—during old age in his wheelchair—showering the deep flower borders with bulbs.

Above: In Gravetye's Little Garden, an intimate space just off the sitting-room, *Berberis thunbergii* 'Atropurpurea Nana' tones with red valerian (*Centranthus ruber*), purple sage (*Salvia purpurea*), the grey-leaved, white daisy, *Anthemis punctata* subsp. *cupaniana*, and the tall, grey ornamental artichoke, *Cynara cardunculus*. *Opposite:* Gravetye Manor, the Elizabethan house that was home to William Robinson. Today it is a glorious country house hotel.

Andrew Russell and chef Mark Raffan. With many years of Gravetye tradition behind them, both are perfectly placed to carry on the traditions and the magic.

The 18 hectares of garden is best explored starting from the north lawn where, towards the end of his life, Robinson often sat in his wheelchair to scatter bulbs into the deep perennial borders.

Robinson planned the garden at Gravetye to be memorable in each season. The famous wild garden begins its parade with the blooming of cowslips, wild orchids and buttercups. 'The term "Wild Garden",' wrote Robinson in *The English Flower Garden* (p. 154), 'has nothing to do with the "wilderness" … it is best explained by the winter Aconite flowering under a grove of naked trees in February; by the Snowflake abundant in meadows by the Thames; and by the Apennine Anemone staining an English grove blue.'

In April, the magnolias unfurl their scented, creamy blooms; they are underplanted with snowdrops, including *Leucojum aestivum* 'Gravetye Giant'. Bluebells and fritillaries push through the cold earth.

In May, the scent of Ghent azaleas and wisteria is overwhelming and during summer the garden beds fill with a tantalising mix of *Dianthus*, *Geranium*, *Artemisia*, *Gypsophila* and *Saliva*, and canes of soft pink, sweetly scented old-fashioned roses arch over wide edgings of York stone. By high summer the borders burst with luscious roses, fat delphiniums and opulent peonies.

The 1-hectare walled kitchen garden is resplendent with produce. Laid out in the style of a potager, with edgings of herbs and strawberries, and flowers for the house planted between rows of vegetables, the kitchen garden is 3 degrees Celsius warmer than any other section of the grounds. It is dressed with aged manure; mushroom compost, which contains lime, is used sparingly.

Bamboo tripods form a spine that supports sweet peas, sugar snap peas, broad beans and French climbing beans. There are gooseberries, white, black and red currents and the raspberry 'Autumn Bliss'—all are made into jams for breakfast and afternoon tea.

Beds of lilies and iris, along with yarrow (*Achillea* spp.) to attract bees, are interspersed with a variety of potatoes including 'Rattes', 'Charlotte', 'Pink Fir Apple' and 'Desiree', which are rotated each year. Fennel is planted with gladiolus and purple-headed alliums, and edged with thyme, purple basil and nasturtiums.

Wedge-shaped beds house countless varieties of lettuce, bordered by spicy rocket and highlighted by horseradish, celeriac and blue-flowering borage, also loved by the bees.

At the centre of many of England's best gardens—including Sissinghurst, High Beeches, Nymans, Great Dixter and the Manor House at Upton Grey—Gravetye provides the perfect focus for a horticultural pilgrimage.

Opposite, top: Wildflower meadows above the lake at Gravetye. ***Opposite, bottom:*** A walk to the lake—through a stone pergola of white *Wisteria sinensis* and golden climbing hop (*Humulus lupulus* 'Aureus') and across the meadows of wildflowers—leads over a rustic bridge to the woodland of ancient oak, beech and maple, and back up to the summer border. ***Above, left:*** The 1-hectare vegetable garden was created in 1898 and remains in full production today. Unlike most Victorian vegetable gardens, which are square, this south-facing garden is elliptical, to provide even light and—nineteenth-century gardeners thought—deny pests and diseases corners in which to multiply. Kiwi fruit, grapes, currants and teaberries are espaliered against the stone walls. ***Above, centre:*** Woven willow hurdles edge beds of berries. ***Above, right:*** There is an ancient asparagus bed and another of globe artichokes, for early summer. A section is also devoted to rhubarb, which is forced in the dark microclimate of ceramic Cretan jars.

Upton Grey

AND THE GARDENS OF

Hestercombe

Art is the expression of man's pleasure in labour.

BRITISH WRITER AND ARTIST WILLIAM MORRIS (1834–1896)

The Manor House at Upton Grey

Imagine stumbling across a country house, clearly architecturally important, but sadly neglected and overrun with weeds; then, soon after months of agonising negotiation and the final exchange of contracts, you discover it possesses a provenance rarer and more precious than you could have dreamed possible.

In 1983, after Rosamund and John Wallinger had bought the Manor House in the English village of Upton Grey, Hampshire, they visited the Institute of Architects in London to research the Edwardian property.

They discovered the house was built by the architect Ernest Newton for Charles Holme on the bones of an old Tudor farmhouse. Holme (1848–1923) was a textile merchant, publisher, plant collector and influential Arts and Crafts figure. They also learnt that during construction, Newton discovered cannon shot from Cromwellian times in the original walls and a bag of seventeenth-century coins in one of the massive chimneys. And then the Wallingers noticed a footnote: 'Garden possibly G. Jekyll'. Thus began an exhilarating journey of discovery and recreation that has continued over almost three decades. Today the garden is meticulously restored—using the original nineteen numbered plans that reside at the University of California, Berkeley campus—and is now considered the most authentic Jekyll garden in the world.

Opposite: You leave Upton Grey's expansive gravel forecourt that folds out from the Manor House and—through a detailed iron gate and past a border of voluptuous peonies, *Paeonia officinalis* 'Rubra Plena'—enter its wild garden of ancient daffodils, old roses and century-old trees.

Gertrude Jekyll (*see* page 30) designed the garden in 1908 for Holme. To their delight, the Wallingers discovered that the skeleton of the 2-hectare garden was intact and salvageable.

The garden begins with beautifully crafted wrought-iron gates that open to the gravel forecourt of the house. From here wide, shallow grass steps (a Jekyll signature) lead to the wild garden. Winding paths snake through uncut grass that houses wildflowers and drifts of original daffodils, identified by the Royal Horticultural Society— 'Horsefield', 'Emperor' and 'Empress'—exactly where Jekyll planted them near a century-old copper beech.

Jekyll's favourite roses were also found in the wild garden—'Dundee Rambler', 'The Garland', 'Blush Rambler'—and, further from the house, species roses such as *R. virginiana,* with its red stems in autumn, and *R. arvensis,* a rambling rose with single white blooms and golden stamens.

The formal garden stretches beyond the house and is retained on several levels by exquisite walls of both Purbeck and Bargate stone. The first level, the rose lawn, is planted with early Hybrid Teas, like the elegant pink *R.* 'Mme Caroline Testout', 'Mme Abel Chatenay' and the climbing 'Lady Waterlow', bred in 1903. They are interplanted with Jekyll's beloved peonies and her adored iris. In the centre of each lawn is a stone square, surrounded by a seat, cleverly designed to house changing pots of scented lilium or brilliantly coloured canna.

This lovely garden starts to waken in February, when the ancient daffodil hybrids and wildflowers follow winter's blue *Iris stylosa.* Then in March the walls drip with a collection of flowering, self-seeding plants, before the borders of bearded iris come to life in late spring and the roses and peonies herald summer.

The Manor House at Upton Grey is beautiful, however, in any month—evidence of a work of passion, artistry and skill, and great intellectual endeavour. As Rosamund Wallinger says in her book, *Gertrude Jekyll's Lost Garden: The Restoration of an Edwardian Masterpiece* (p. 19), 'At no stage in the restoration of her masterpiece have I wanted to change any part. I have remained a contented disciple.'

The Gardens of Hestercombe

A few hours south-west of Upton Grey, another great Jekyll garden, Hestercombe, has been restored with a £3.7 million Heritage Lottery Grant. Situated near Taunton, Somerset, Hestercombe was laid out as a landscape garden in the 1750s by the artist Coplestone Warre Bampfylde: his mother's family had owned the estate since the fourteenth century.

In 1904 the then owner Edward Portman commissioned Edwin Lutyens and Gertrude Jekyll to create a formal Edwardian garden, which was completed in 1908. It is largely to this incarnation that the garden has now been restored, utilising the copy of Jekyll's planting plans, which were given at the time to Hestercombe's head gardener and were recently found in a drawer in a potting shed. The plans, specifying plant varieties in Jekyll's hand, are now held at the University of California, Berkley campus, after the American landscape

Top: Upton Grey, an Elizabethan house, seen from the picking garden, where delphiniums, lupins and lavender flower with clematis and roses. ***Bottom, left:*** Upton Grey's terraced garden is retained by stone walls, where catmint (*Nepeta mussinii*) and the yellow-flowering *Aurinia saxatalis* (syn. *Alyssum saxatile*) make themselves at home. Peonies, lavenders and roses jostle for position in the wide borders. ***Bottom, right:*** Viewed from across the wild garden: St Mary's Upton Grey. The church dates from the twelfth century, and the tower was added in 1690. Jekyll placed garden seats at points from which she wished the garden to be enjoyed. She also believed that seats should be unobtrusive. 'The common habit of painting garden seats a dead white is certainly open to criticism,' she wrote. 'The seat should not be made too conspicuous. Like all other painted things about a garden: gates, railings, or flower-tubs, the painting should be such as to suit the environment; it should in no case be so glaring as to draw almost exclusive attention to itself.'

GERTRUDE JEKYLL

Gertrude Jekyll (1843–1932) was already an acknowledged artist and craftswoman, skilled in embroidery, woodwork, silversmithing and photography, when deteriorating eyesight and a consultation with an eye specialist in 1891 encouraged her interest in gardening and garden design.

A chance meeting two years earlier in May 1889 with the twenty-year-old architect Edwin Lutyens (1869–1944), when Jekyll (her name rhymes with 'treacle') was 46, resulted in a design collaboration that left a legacy of more than 400 commissions: gardens of exuberant plantings constrained within the formality of a clear, strong structure that has contributed to their endurance over many decades.

Jekyll's lasting influence was due to her skill in seamlessly combining several gardening styles, as well as her advanced ideas on colour and texture. Her designs also employed the structure and scale of the gardens of the Italian Renaissance, which she had admired in her travels. Water and stone, along with the greys of Mediterranean plants, were used to great effect in her gardens.

Jekyll's diverse talents came together at her home, Munstead Wood, designed by Lutyens in the architectural vernacular of her village, Godalming. Here Jekyll's garden became the laboratory for her ideas. In the sandy, acidic Surrey soil, her fascination with plant combinations and the intricate weaving of colour, texture and shape, influenced by the impressionist painters of the era, resulted in voluptuous flower borders, which changed with each season.

She planted in drifts, skilfully grading hues and tints, which interested her more than exotic plants brought back by energetic plant hunters of the time. She was expert in arranging plants so that one would drape over another reaching the end of its flowering season. She grew hydrangeas, dahlias, Michaelmas daisies, lilies and iris in pots, ready to pop into a space in the garden, so that her main borders were always in perfect condition.

Her woodlands of Scots pine, chestnut, oak and birch remain at Munstead Wood, underplanted with azaleas and rhododendrons and through which simple grass paths meander. Small 'rooms' carpeted in stone are detailed with a tapestry of hostas, francoas, begonias and other plants admired for the tone and texture of their foliage.

By the time she died, Jekyll had published a dozen books, the first of which, *Wood and Garden*, was released in 1899. This was followed by *Wall & Water Gardens*, *Roses for English Gardens* and *Gardens for Small Country Houses*. She also contributed almost 1000 articles to magazines, including *Country Life*, which was launched in England in 1897. Jekyll wrote for *Gardening Illustrated* and *The Garden*—the creation of her friend William Robinson, who became renowned as the father of a wild, or more relaxed, style of gardening (*see* pages 21–5).

In a conversation in June 2004, her biographer Michael Tooley said of Jekyll, 'She was up to date … not old fashioned. She was using new plants from all over the world, using them in the gardens and then writing about them. She was the person who said how do you link the house with the garden; she taught Lutyens.'

architect Beatrix Farrand—who had bought 'the entire output of Gertrude Jekyll's long and distinguished career'—bequeathed them to the university.

Lutyens's and Jekyll's love of the Italian Renaissance gardens, with their reliance on stone and water, is clearly demonstrated at Hestercombe, where the architect's disciplined, geometric plans are softened by the intricate weaving of colour, texture and shape in Jekyll's sensuous plantings.

Today the garden is entered by the eighteenth-century landscape garden walk, which continues past the beautiful, pear-shaped lake, with its cascades and plantings of moisture-loving species, and through the woodland.

A Lutyens-designed chinoiserie gate links this earlier garden with its Edwardian partner and leads to the East Garden, now in its original costume through meticulous reconstruction, using Jekyll's planting plans. This stone terrace, bound on one side by an elegant orangery, is planted with extensive sweeps of water-wise Mediterranean plants: lavender, valerian, rosemary and the grey-leaved *Stachys*. The much-photographed terracotta urns, filled with cascading catmint, add—along with the rich cream spires of *Yucca*—height and importance to this area.

Opposite: Gertrude Jekyll's home, Munstead Wood, designed by Sir Edwin Lutyens in her village, Godalming, Surrey. *Top:* Perhaps the most dramatic section of Hestercombe's garden, which represents the Lutyens–Jekyll collaboration at its most grand, is the Great Plat, an expansive, sunken parterre laid out in formal sections, each edged in flat stone and packed with lilies, delphiniums and peonies. Along the entire length of the parterre, which affords extensive views over the Vale of Taunton, is a stone pergola, covered in a glorious tangle of climbing roses, honeysuckle and clematis. *Above, left:* Stone was central to Jekyll's designs. *Above, centre:* The lake at Hestercombe. *Above, right:* Hestercombe flowerbeds are edged in stone.

Jekyll's Grey Walk, sited beneath the grand terrace that fronts the house, is an exquisite tonal wave of whites, greys and silvers to lilacs and blues, all painted in easygoing lavenders, iris, phlomis, santolinas and teucriums.

This is an exhilarating garden and, even though not many of us will own gardens as grand as Hestercombe, there is much here to teach and inspire: Jekyll's clever framing of vistas, her virtuoso use of colour, scale and symmetry, her design of steps and edgings in stone, and her myriad ways to embrace water. A paradise, indeed.

> *The more permanent materials of which the [Italian garden] is made—the stonework, the evergreen foliage, the effects of rushing or motionless water—all form part of the artist's design. But ... the inherent beauty of the garden lies in the grouping of its parts—in the converging lines of long ilex walks, the alternation of sunny open spaces with cool woodland shade, the proportion ... between the height of a wall or the width of a path.*
>
> **EDITH WHARTON, *ITALIAN VILLAS AND THEIR GARDENS*, P. 8**

Opposite: The many flights of steps—some broad, some straight, some semi-circular, but all shallow, as Jekyll dictated—which connect the different areas and varying levels of Hestercombe's intricate garden, are constructed from the local silver-grey slate, softened by self-sown, blue-flowering convolvulus, white snow-in-summer (*Cerastium tomentosum*), erigeron and wallflowers. *Above:* On either side of Hestercombe's main terrace raised grass walks are dissected by narrow rills, edged in stone, and filled with iris, arum lilies and skunk cabbage. These are known as the East and West Rills, and each culminate in a sunken pool fed by a mask spouting water from intricately constructed stone alcoves.

Zhuozheng Yuan

(THE HUMBLE ADMINISTRATOR'S GARDEN)

Given a piece of ground, no matter if it be small, and devoid of natural beauty ... they will patiently transform it into a mountain-landscape in miniature. With strange-looking weather-worn rocks, dwarfed trees, bamboo, herbs and water, a piece of wild countryside is evolved, replete with mountain and stream, forest and field, plateau and lake, grotto and dell.

PLANT HUNTER ERNEST WILSON IN PETER VALDER, *GARDENS IN CHINA*, P. 50

A couple of hours south-west of Shanghai on the lower reaches of the Yangtze River in Jiangsu Province lies Suzhou, a city that dates back to the sixth century, and today is home to a population of some six million. Lying on the Grand Canal—which was built in the seventh century from Beijing south to Hangzhou to facilitate trade and commerce—Suzhou is renowned for its old quarter of heritage buildings, silk production, pearls and gardens.

Traditional Chinese gardens sought to represent, in miniature, a wider landscape; to reflect a desire to live in harmony with nature, rather than to conquer it. Along with poetry, painting and calligraphy, garden-making was once the preserve of the educated—rulers, nobles and officials. Long before the Chinese garden matured to reach its greatest artifice and ornamentation—perhaps during the Southern Song Period (1127–1279)—its incarnation was as a game park, the domain of the ruling class. The privately owned gardens of the Song Period, largely belonging to government officials, were concentrated in the south of China, around the cities of Wuxi, Suzhou and Hangzhou.

Opposite: Hangzhou, close to Suzhou, is today one of China's most beautiful cities. The city's West Lake, set against mist-covered mountains, has long inspired artists and writers, revered as nature's model for garden-making. During the Southern Song Period, when the imperial court transferred here, the lake provided a sublime setting for palaces and classical gardens.

Top, left: Small garden art pieces were particularly important in Chinese private gardens, which were not as expansive as imperial landscapes. *Top, centre*: In the gardens of scholar officials—such as Liu Yuan, or the Garden to Linger In, in Suzhou—the peony is revered. *Top, right*: Wild apricots (*Prunus armeniaca*) flourish on the hillsides below the Great Wall. *Above*: The Humble Administrator's Garden is designed around a languid, meandering pond. As instructed by the garden designer, poet and painter Ji Cheng in his three-volume treatise on landscape practice and theory, *Yuan Ye* or *The Craft of Gardens*, the pool occupies some one-third of the garden. *Opposite, top*: Long grown in Chinese gardens, weeping willows—with their flexible form and branches—symbolise feminine beauty and grace. *Opposite, bottom*: The Chinese snowball tree, *Viburnum macrocephalum*.

Among the best known of the private Chinese gardens is Zhuozheng Yuan or the Humble Administrator's Garden. It was built in 1509 on the site of a former temple during the prosperous Ming Dynasty (1368–1644) by Wang Xianchen, a retired government official. Like many Chinese intellectuals, an engagement with nature accompanied his literary and artistic talents.

Today a UNESCO World Heritage site, the garden covers some 5 hectares and is divided into several sections to incorporate hills, dense bamboo and pine forests, and winding streams. One-third of the central section of the garden is a languid pond, lined with pavilions featuring evocative names: the Hall of Distant Fragrance and the Celestial Spring Pavilion. There is also the Fragrant Snow and Clouds Pavilion, set on a small clearing on the peak of a hill, as well as the enchanting Lotus Breeze from All Sides. One ornate hall houses camellias; another cymbidium orchids.

An eighth of the world's plants—some 31 000 species—are native to China and many we now take for granted hail from this vast land. Chinese gardens, however—like those in Japan, to where their influence spread—rely upon a restricted horticultural palette.

Two types of indigenous pines are most often used: the rough-barked *Pinus tabuliformis* (Chinese red pine), which assumes a horizontal, flat crown when mature, and *Pinus bungeana* (lacebark pine), with its smooth trunk reminiscent of some Australian eucalypts. Magnolias and viburnums are prized; while the delicate branches of the weeping willow often provide

a soft background, and the exuberant blossom of the pear and peach herald springtime. The common Chinese lilac (*Syringa oblata*) is preferred over a more flamboyant hybrid, and species roses, like the single yellow *R. xanthina*, are often used in hedges.

A close connection with, and appreciation of, the changing seasons pervades life in China, where each month of the year and each season is accorded a plant. Pine, plum blossom and bamboo traditionally signify winter: pine because of its endurance, gnarled bark and scent of its needles; plum blossom because it appears on bare branches in the dark depths of winter; and bamboo because it remains evergreen. Bamboo is hollow with humility, depicting gentleness; it bends in the wind to rise again when the storm has abated. The camellia heralds spring, the lotus and the revered peony are associated with summer, while the chrysanthemum represents autumn.

Tracing the route by which plants such as the tea rose, peony, daphne, viburnum, mock orange and magnolia travelled from China to the horticultural world makes a fascinating study, just as the movement of plants into China from states close by—including Manchuria, Korea and Japan to the north—reflects the sometimes turbulent history of the region. Plants also arrived into China from the Middle East, probably through Iran; and Portuguese and Spanish ships, particularly after the sixteenth century, called at ports in Guangdong and Fujian Provinces, bringing with them species from the Americas. Chinese plants, tea, spices and other commodities found their way onto these ships for the return journey.

The greatest export of plants from China occurred after the last decades of the eighteenth century, largely through the efforts of the plant hunters, many from the United Kingdom. Searching for botanical trophies for a plant-hungry public back home, plant hunters courted great danger throughout China, the Himalayas and Tibet in their quest for the exotic and rare that exemplified the mysteries behind closed borders. Among the most intrepid was Ernest 'Chinese' Wilson (1876–1930), whose adventures make for exciting and terrifying reading.

The richness and diversity of the ancient private gardens in China are well demonstrated in Suzhou, where the gardens of scholar-officials also remain to remind us of the importance placed upon intellectual and artistic pursuits. In these gardens the ideals of emulating the perfection of nature, and its rivers, streams, waterfalls and mountains, reached its greatest artistry.

Opposite, top: Exercise, part of the Chinese engagement with nature, is taken on one of the islands in the Humble Administrator's Garden.
Opposite, bottom: The Humble Administrator's Garden is divided into three sections representing the idyllic charm of nature.

Above, left to right:
Pinus tabuliformis is one of the two indigenous pines most often used in Chinese gardens.

Roses have been recorded in Chinese gardens for some 3000 years and have always played an important part in Chinese art. The single yellow *Rosa xanthina*—a wild form of *Rosa hugonis*, the Golden Rose of China—was sent to Britain from China in 1899.

Bamboo, pine and plum: the three friends of winter in Beijing's Zhongshan Park. These three plants are central to the Chinese aesthetic, seen repeatedly in painting, literature and garden design.

A rich cerise peony at Liu Yuan.

A hybrid tree peony.

Rock-work in the central section of the Humble Administrator's Garden: rocks, symbolic of human spirituality and an understanding of nature, conjure images of the mist-shrouded mountain peaks of a wider landscape and—as in the Japanese aesthetic—are also associated with immortality.

A SENSE OF PLACE

Great art—whether manifest in exquisite, handmade textiles or on a canvas washed with the light of a summer evening—and great music can move us to tears. A perfectly formed rose, rich in colour and heady with scent, can also elicit deep emotion, as can a superb garden. And what is it about a pristine wilderness, such as an alpine meadow, that can overwhelm us with its beauty? It is sometimes difficult to articulate what it is that makes a garden—or a landscape—great, but you recognise it when you find it. A sense of place—the *genius loci*—is surely the most important, and the most elusive, element in the creation of a beautiful garden.

Ninfa

One sees clearly only with the heart. Anything essential is invisible to the eyes.

FRENCH WRITER ANTOINE DE SAINT EXUPÉRY (1900–1944)

The picturesque gardens of the ruined medieval town of Ninfa lie slumbering in the shadow of the towering Lepini Mountains, about an hour south of Rome. Ninfa was once the thriving site of a crennelated castle within double city walls, a town hall, six churches, numerous houses, bakeries and a blacksmith. It has an old and venerable history, dating at least to the first century, when Pliny the Younger recorded a visit to the Temple of the Nymphs, which gave the town its name.

Built on the edge of a fast-flowing river at the foot of Sermoneta, a golden Etruscan hill town, and at the edge of the Pontine Marshes, Ninfa was acquired in 1297 by the aristocratic Pietro Caetani. Close to the Via Appia, the town was a resting place for travellers, and commerce was brisk. In 1382 the town was destroyed when the family opposed the pope in the religious struggles of the time, and any townspeople who survived fled. Ninfa lay deserted and crumbling for hundreds of years, although it remained well known for its botanical collections.

Then, almost a century ago, members of the Caetani family reclaimed their lands and set about stabilising the ruins—some of which were still

Opposite, left: The romantic gardens of the ruined medieval town of Ninfa lie in the shadow of the Lepini Mountains below the Etruscan hill town, Sermoneta.
Left: Conifers soar towards the light, playing host to roses such as *R. filipes*, which tumbles like a veil of fine netting, flowering in white clusters.

decorated with the remains of Byzantine frescoes—replenishing the gardens and rejuvenating the waterways.

Assisted by benign winter temperatures, hot summers and abundant water from the hills behind, which is stored in huge reservoirs, Ninfa is now a 12-hectare plantsman's paradise, home to exotic species from all over the world. Today there is no surface that doesn't support cascades of roses, wisteria and jasmine; these drip down the ancient, mellow walls and romp up stately cypress, although the medieval layout of the ancient town is still visible in the ruined city walls and buildings.

There are collections of dogwoods, maples, viburnums, and the graceful, weeping ribbonwood (*Hoheria sexstylosa*), with its scented, white flowers, native to New Zealand. There are tulip trees (*Liriodendron tulipifera*) from North America and the primeval maidenhair tree (*Ginkgo biloba*), a living fossil only introduced to the western world from China in the last century. In 1976 almost 2000 hectares of Ninfa's land were set aside as a protected reserve for wildlife.

Opposite, top: There are few surfaces at Ninfa that are not covered in vines or roses.
Opposite, bottom: A stone bridge is festooned with long racemes of *Wisteria floribunda* 'Macrobotrys' in May, and in June with roses. Groves of *Magnolia × soulangeana* also flower in pink goblets in late spring, when smoke bush, *Cotinus coggygria* 'Flame', blooms like fairy floss above russet-coloured leaves.
Top, left to right: The castle tower rises from the remaining town walls, overlooked by Etruscan hill towns. *Above:* The giant rhubarb, *Gunnera manicata*, erupts from frozen earth each spring.

Above, left: Ninfa's tower rises from the ancient city walls. *Above, centre left:* The stone bridge dates from Roman times. *Above, centre right:* A double avenue of lavender leads to the walls of the medieval town. The often flat-topped stone pine (*Pinus pinea*) is a familiar sight in Italy's landscape. *Above, right:* Roses envelop crumbling walls. *Opposite, top:* An old rose seedling, probably 'American Pillar', rambles across Ninfa's venerable walls. *Opposite, bottom:* As the Ninfa River meanders through the gardens, iris, oyster plant, magnolias and wild roses bloom over many months, in the shadows of the mountains and hill towns.

This romantic garden is somewhat English in its emotional appeal, perhaps appearing more natural than many of the gardens you might encounter in Italy. But while the gardens of the Italian Renaissance were based upon linear severity along with virtuoso water features that were aligned to a central axis, an appreciation of the surrounding landscape was also important to the landscapers of the time. Ninfa, an entrancing garden of mystery and intrigue, of constant scents, sounds and colour, certainly respects its *genius loci*.

In the dark days of World War II, the owners Roffredo Caetani and his American wife, Marguerite, (the Duke and Duchess of Sermoneta) held open house for friends—artists, writers, diplomats, politicians and travellers—many of whom left written records of the gardens. From La Foce, her garden near Sienna, writer Iris Origo noted of their hospitality:

> Here, on Sundays, Roffredo and Marguerite kept open house for an extremely varied collection of guests: foreign diplomats and men of letters, elegant Roman ladies and Englishwomen with stout boots and an expert knowledge of gardening, bearded young painters or musicians and classical scholars from the American Academy, eminent foreign statesmen and rising young politicians.

LES
Jardins
DU
Paradis

In Cordes, everything is beautiful, even regret.

ALBERT CAMUS (1913–1960), FRENCH AUTHOR, PHILOSOPHER AND RECIPIENT OF THE
NOBEL PRIZE FOR LITERATURE, UPON VISITING CORDES-SUR-CIEL IN THE 1950S

About a twenty-minute drive from the historic town of Albi in the Tarn region of south-west France, and some 70 kilometres north of Toulouse, the fortified town of Cordes-sur-Ciel perches atop a rocky hill, little changed since its establishment in 1222. Built to protect the population of the surrounding rural area from attack, the town escaped severe damage during the religious wars of the sixteenth century. As a result, excellent examples of thirteenth- and fourteenth-century gothic architecture have been preserved, with many of the inhabitants still living in houses built within the ancient ramparts.

This part of France seems to have escaped the worst of the tourist born scourges of appalling traffic, sky-high prices and disappointing coffee that can afflict the more well-known areas—at least in summer. The Tarn is a farming region, rich in gourmet traditions, replete with villages built of mellow local stone and, once you know where to look, some fascinating gardens.

One is Les Jardins du Paradis, which was laid out in 1998 on a steep hillside in the old section of Cordes by two plantsmen and designers, Eric Ossart and Arnaud Maurières. Like other gardens that are intended to reflect an imagined paradise—in accordance with the gardens created from the time of the emergence of the Persian Empire (*see* pages 3–7)— Les Jardins du Paradis comprises a series of enclosures, some large and

Opposite: An iron arbour forms a boundary on one side of the vegetable garden in Les Jardins du Paradis. The very double pink rose 'Louise Odier' climbs in company with 'The Fairy' and 'Ballerina'. At their feet, the Hybrid Tea 'Lavender Dream' jostles with the heavily scented, butterfly-attracting *Buddleja* 'Black Knight'.

Above: These cascades of galvanised iron buckets form a witty water feature to lead the visitor onto the middle level at Les Jardins du Paradis. *Opposite, top*: Dawn lights the hill town of Cordes-sur-Ciel, in the south-west of France. *Opposite, centre*: The design of the intricate picking garden was inspired by the Persian carpet. The woven willow screen allows glimpses into the different sections of the garden. *Opposite, bottom*: The hot section of the picking garden: here yellow daylilies team with red hot pokers and euphorbias.

some small, but each a place for rest and contemplation. The entire garden, on three terraces, covers some 3500 square metres.

This is a garden of surprise, excitement and inspiration. It is entered through a cloister, designed in four sections, and filled with blue-flowering perennials arranged around a large square of thyme, from which a water sculpture erupts. The walls are clothed in a deep blue clematis and fragrant moonflowers, and paths are of broken slate, adding colour and sound to the space.

A flight of stone steps, protected on one side by a stone wall inset with pots of black-leaved oxalis, takes you past a series of iron buckets, which serves as an extremely attractive cascade and fountain—a tribute to the water that is crucial to the success of this garden and central to the paradise gardens of ancient Persia.

On the middle level a cool enclave of lush bananas, enclosed in a tall box hedge, provides another surprise. Although they will withstand temperatures to -15 degrees Celsius, the bananas are protected by hessian shrouds from frosts during the severe winters experienced in the region. Paulownias, annually coppiced into a living pergola, provide summer shade.

Gravel paths lead to the picking gardens, divided into three 'rooms' of different colourways, each separated by a woven willow screen that affords enticing glimpses from one area

to the next. Designed as a floral tapestry inspired by the Persian carpet, this section employs sequences of perennials and annuals to ensure continual flowering as well as exciting colour, texture and shape.

In the first enclosure the tall-growing, deep-blue-to-purple *Verbena bonariensis,* along with Russian sage (*Perovskia atriplicifolia*), the pastel *Nicotiana alata*, species geraniums, aquilegias and iris clothe the garden in blues, greys, creams and whites. Ground-covers are the blue-flowering *Ajuga reptans* 'Bugle Boy' and thyme.

In the next square the hot garden explodes with yellow and orange kniphofias, yellow and red day lilies, the sprawling, fast-growing, intensely yellow *Cosmos sulphureus* 'Klondike' and the bright yellow, fluffy flowerheads of dill.

The third enclosure holds a collection of grasses: the tall, striped *Miscanthus sinensis* 'Zebrinus', the deep red Japanese blood grass, and swaths of grey-green festucas and curling bronze carex.

On the lower terrace a high screen of espaliered apples forms the perimeter of the garden. Paths covered in terracotta shards provide a carpet for pots of frothy pink roses— 'The Fairy' and 'Ballerina'—which are shaded by an iron arbour covered in the deep pink rose 'Louise Odier'.

On this level a collection of antique vegetables is housed in a series of raised beds edged with aged sleepers to ensure ease of maintenance. As well as a variety of old-fashioned tomatoes and a vast selection of herbs, there is the maize-like *Coix lacryma-jobi* for bread-making and borage to attract bees, essential for pollination throughout the garden. *Indigofera tinctoria,* a deciduous perennial traded since ancient times throughout the Middle East and northern Africa, is grown for the blue dye extracted from its leaves.

The five senses are fully employed in this garden, from the crunch of terracotta, slate and gravel paths and soft music of the water features to the visual excitement of brilliant colours and the perfumes of flowers.

Opposite: At the entrance, a small room is designed to engage all the senses—from the crunch of broken terracotta pots underfoot to the scent of climbing plants.

> *We travel for years without really knowing what we're looking for ... then all of a sudden we stumble on one of the two or three places in the world that are waiting for each of us. We arrive and finally our heart is at rest and we understand that we have arrived. The traveller who, from the terraces of Cordes, looks up at the sky at night in the summer knows that he need go no further and that here, if he wants, the beauty of the surroundings will day after day remove all feelings of loneliness.*

ALBERT CAMUS IN CLAIRE TARGUEBAYRE, *CORDES EN ABIGEOIS,* **P. II**

Cottesbrooke Hall

Thou still unravish'd bride of quietness,
Thou foster-child of Silence and slow Time,
Sylvan historian, who canst thus express
A flowery tale more sweetly than our rhyme:
What leaf-fringed legend haunts about thy shape
Of deities or mortals, or of both,
In Tempe or the dales of Arcady?

JOHN KEATS, 'ODE ON A GRECIAN URN', VERSE 1, LINES 1–7

Northamptonshire, the region at the heart of England, is as undiscovered as it is lovely. An area of gently rolling hills, its beauty is somewhat understated: soft and kind. The area abounds in charming market towns, thatched cottages and magnificent churches. That Northamptonshire is also the site of some of England's best gardens is a bonus.

The building of Cottesbrooke Hall, an exquisite house of pink brick and local stone, began in 1702 during the reign of Queen Anne and around the time that many other wonderful houses, including Chatsworth, Duncombe Park and Castle Howard, were being created. The original architect of this elegant house, with its refined detailing, is unknown; in 1780 Robert Mitchell added the lovely east and west bows to the central block, as well as the bridge by which the public enters the property, and

Opposite: In the formal gardens at Cottesbrooke Hall, the Dog Gates—which reflect the family's interest in country sports—lead through to the Pool Garden. The stylish copper-domed shade house was designed by eminent landscape designer Dame Sylvia Crowe.

Above: Cottesbrooke Hall is approached by its elegant bridge, built in 1780 by the architect Robert Mitchell. **Opposite:** The north terrace, shaded by a pair of ancient *Cedrus libani*, boasts mirrored perennial borders. The performance begins in May and continues through summer to peak in September. The lime greens of *Alchemilla mollis* are teamed with *Allium* 'Purple Sensation', and black tulips contrast with tall, yellow lupins. Clematis and sweet peas climb on pea-stick tripods of hazel.

from where the house is best viewed. Jane Austen scholars maintain that the house was the setting for *Mansfield Park*, the author's most 'landscaped' novel.

The 3.5 hectares of formal, detailed gardens have largely been developed during the twentieth century, with the help of several distinguished landscape designers, including Sir Geoffrey Jellicoe (1900–1996) and Dame Sylvia Crowe (1901–1997). The present owner's grandmother, the late Lady Catherine Macdonald-Buchanan, was a major force in creating one of England's most exciting gardens. This is grand, masterful gardening, which manages simultaneously to maintain a joyful and intimate feel.

The house is sited on an axis with the distant spire of Brixworth Church, which was built in 680 AD, some 1.5 kilometres to the south. The parterre and forecourt in front of the house

were laid out by Jellicoe in 1938: there are high stumpy yews, statues set in formal rose beds of white 'Pascali' and a stone balustrade rising behind massive walls of box hedges. From here, magnificent vistas of the 250 hectares of parkland, lakes and bridges open out.

To the west is the Sculpture Walk, dominated by early eighteenth-century works by Peter Scheemakers (1691–1781), a Dutchman who arrived in England around 1730 and became one of its leading sculptors. A series of small, intimate gardens—enclosed by either high walls or hedges and filled with a palette of special plants (wisteria, magnolias, rare tulips, swaths of primulas and collections of hostas)—folds out from here before the woodland garden makes way for the beautiful park.

Opposite, top: *Wisteria floribunda* 'Kuchi-beni' adorns the west wing. *Opposite, bottom*: The house extends from a central hall with east and west elevations, added in 1780 by Robert Mitchell. *Top*: Cottesbrooke Hall's beautiful park. *Above, left*: Eagle gates lead to the Pool Garden. *Above, centre*: In the Wild Garden, rhododendrons, azaleas and bluebells flourish under towering copper beech, larch, bird cherry, Japanese maple and Atlantic cedar. *Above, right*: The Sculpture Walk exhibits works by Peter Scheemakers.

Thuya Garden

Lead through the park, where lines of trees unite,
And verdurous lawns the bounding deer delight:
By gentle falls the docile ground descends,
Forms a fair plain, then by degrees ascends.
These inequalities delight the eye,
For nature charms most in variety ...
O'er all designs Nature should still preside:
She is the cheapest and most perfect guide.

ANNE INGRAM, LADY IRWIN (C. 1696–1764), 'CASTLE HOWARD,
THE SEAT OF THE RT HON. CHARLES, EARL OF CARLISLE'

The wild and beautiful coast along the state of Maine, on the east side of the United States, and a few hours' drive north of Boston, also harbours innumerable sheltered, calm bays. There are old-time fishing villages with quaint shops and narrow streets—one, Camden, is the setting for the television series *Murder She Wrote*—as well as rugged cliffs covered in picturesque stands of endemic conifers and national parks of untouched wilderness.

The Maine coast remains a warm-weather playground for much of eastern America but probably reached its peak during the so-called Golden Age of gardens, in the late nineteenth and early twentieth centuries, when leading families built massive estates in which to spend the summers. Grand, European-style gardens were created by such landscapers as Beatrix Jones Farrand (1872–1959), who was influenced by the work of the English artist and garden designer Gertrude Jekyll (*see* pages 27–33),

Opposite: Thuya Garden is a place of tall trees, with quiet places for rest and contemplation; the simple design contrasts with the more flamboyant estates of the east coast holiday resorts, which exemplified the Golden Age of American gardens.

Above: The cliffside track up to Thuya Garden affords extraordinary views over Northeast Harbor, Maine. *Opposite, top:* The climb leads through stands of indigenous northern white cedar, *Thuja occidentalis*. *Opposite, bottom:* The formal herbaceous border is filled with all the flowers for cutting you would expect to find in an English garden.

best known for detailed and voluptuous herbaceous borders set within a formal framework of stone steps, paths and balustrades.

At Maine's uber-smart Bar Harbor, Farrand made her own shorefront garden, Reef Point (originally her mother's home), her laboratory and trial ground. Here, she gathered a plant collection soon considered to be the most important north of Boston's famed Arnold Arboretum, where she had trained with its charismatic and didactic director Charles Sprague Sargent (1841–1927).

In 1955, however, perhaps because she realised they could not be maintained after her death as she would wish, Farrand ordered her house and garden to be dismantled. Her collection of plants now rests at Thuya Garden in the nearby village of Northeast Harbor, in the part of Maine known, somewhat whimsically, as 'Downeast and Acadia'.

Situated on the western slope of Eliot Mountain—named after Charles Eliot, president of Harvard University—Thuya Garden is among several extensive gardens in the area that hark back to a privileged era of garden-making. It is part of the Asticou Terraces Preserve, 60 hectares of dark, atmospheric woodlands and walking tracks, the centre of which is an exquisite garden laid out in the style of Jekyll. Thuya Garden is best reached with a little

effort by taking the steps from the eastern shore of Northeast Harbor and climbing up through the stands of indigenous white cedar (*Thuja occidentalis*), which cover the cliffs. There are several lookouts on the way, cut into the rocky mountainside, and these afford gorgeous views over a picture-postcard scene of yachts bobbing in the blue-watered cove below.

The garden and its charming house, built in a simple hunting lodge or 'rusticator' style of the late nineteenth century—harking back to a rugged way of life, before the moneyed bankers and railroad developers arrived in the area—was the summer home of the Boston landscape architect Joseph Henry Curtis. Upon his death in 1928 the grounds, Thuya Lodge—the repository of many important botanical manuscripts—and an endowment were left in trust for the enjoyment of the townspeople and holiday-makers. The Asticou Terraces Trust was formed and local resident and landscape designer Charles Savage was appointed trustee. He enlisted the aid of several well-known locals, including John D Rockefeller Jnr—whose garden, The Eyrie, at nearby Seal Harbor was designed by Farrand—and later purchased all the plants from Farrand's Reef Point garden.

The wonderful garden that Savage created at Thuya pays tribute to Jekyll, in the style so often interpreted by Farrand for coastal Maine. Long, formal herbaceous borders form the basis of the design, arranged to incorporate a cross-axis, and are filled with all the cutting flowers you would expect to see in an English garden. A pavilion for sitting in quiet enjoyment of these lovely gardens lies at one end of the long border; a shallow reflection pool forms the southern point. Rare conifers rest at the edges of wide lawns, and a high fence of the local cedar protects the garden treasures from the wildlife of the surrounding forests.

There is much to explore, and several gardens to visit, along the coast of Maine: Thuya is one that should not be missed.

Opposite, top: Large-scale works from a local potter rest among the green tapestry of conifers in Thuya Garden. *Opposite, centre and bottom:* Asticou Azalea Gardens, where many of the plants from Beatrix Farrand's garden now thrive. In a letter to Charles Savage on 1 June 1956, Farrand wrote, 'It is a comfort to know that the plants from R.P. will continue their lives with you.' *Above, left to right:* Iris 'Nutmeg'; *Gerbera* species; *Lilium lancifolium.*

Bentley

*Perfection is achieved, not when there is nothing more to add,
but when there is nothing left to take away.*

FRENCH WRITER ANTOINE DE SAINT EXUPÉRY (1900–1944)

There are surely few places in the world as beautiful as Tasmania's Chudleigh Valley. Running across the island, from east to west, the valley is flanked by mountains that are clothed in old-growth forests of native beech, stringybark, celerytop pine, satinwood and blackwood, and in which alpine meadows remain pristine. The area is steeped in the history of both Aboriginal and European settlement.

Collector and antique dealer John Hawkins and his wife, artist Robyn Mayo, moved to the valley from the Southern Highlands of New South Wales in 2004, after buying Bentley, part of an 1829 grant of some 400 hectares to a John Badcock Gardiner.

The Hawkins set about renovating the historic homestead, built in 1879, then at the centre of a much larger holding, which had been purchased with the assistance of £20 000 from the Manchester Cotton Company.

The park that the Hawkins have laid out around the nineteenth-century house borrows from English landscape traditions, while respecting, above all, its unique setting in the shadow of the blue-tinged Great Western Tiers, the mountain range that forms a north-south rib through the centre of the island. There are extraordinary views in all directions: west to the Tiers, north to the Gog Range and beyond to the mountains named Roland and Claude by early Europeans, and across fields and flood plains that were once fire-farmed by the local Pallitore Aboriginal people.

A long drive of indigenous mountain white gum (*Eucalyptus dalrympleana*) and the silver banksia (*Banksia marginata*) leads into the property,

Opposite: This cupola was added, as the nineteenth-century house was recently renovated and extended, in lieu of built follies in the Bentley landscape. It rises like a piece of confectionery from the conservatory at the centre of the homestead.

giving way to plantings of oak closer to the house. In order to reinstate some of the skills that had been brought into the valley with European settlement—including the building of drystone walls and traditional hedge laying—John Hawkins brought a craftsman from England to teach local tradesmen over several winters. Now, a wonderful drystone wall, which John has dubbed 'the great wall of Chudleigh', surrounds the park-like garden.

The nineteenth-century house—which has now been doubled in size and to which a decorative cupola has been added—was originally built in the style of a Melbourne town villa, not suitable for the expansive landscape the Hawkins planned for Bentley, and for the sense of place afforded by its location. The Hawkins applied to the Heritage Council to have the landscape listed, therefore, and instead of building follies in the landscape, extended the house as the folly—hence the cupola.

A great deal of regeneration and restoration has taken place during the past few years. Robyn has regenerated the creek that runs from the higher parts of the property, feeding the main east lake. A higher dam, which controls water flow into the creek in times of heavy rain, was renovated and trenches were installed in the creek to ensure it doesn't flood. Dozens of weeping willows (*Salix babylonica*) and the introduced brown bulrush (*Typha*

Opposite, top: At dawn the house is reflected in one of three lakes on the property. *Opposite, bottom*: The late afternoon sun lights Mother Cumming's Peak, named for a local school teacher who, in the nineteenth century, took her class to the top of the mountain. *Top*: The creek that feeds the lakes has been revegetated with indigenous melaleucas, casuarinas, eucalypts, poas and *Juncus* and is now a haven for native birds and endangered frogs. *Above, left*: The Helmut Schwabe sculpture. *Above, centre*: The Great Western Tiers, which run north–south through the centre of Tasmania, rise behind the property. *Above, right*: The stone barn was once a staging post on the access route further west.

THE LOGGING DEBATE

An issue that continues to create heated debate in Tasmania is the clearfell logging of old-growth forests and the logging of forests of high conservation value—both crucial as natural regulators of carbon dioxide—throughout the island state. In 1985 the state government created a system perhaps unique to Tasmania—the private timber reserve (PTR) system—which allows private landowners to log their forests. This system removes authority from local councils—which were becoming increasingly concerned about logging and plantation establishment—thus removing landowners from the jurisdiction of their local planning authority. The system requires a landowner to apply to Private Forests Tasmania for their land to be assessed, and then to advertise that they are in possession of a private timber reserve. Once approval is given, the landowner is free to use the land as they wish, including clearfelling it, mainly to supply the state's voracious wood-chipping industry, which demands more than three million tonnes of timber annually.

Many old-time loggers advocate continued, sustainable selective logging of the state's forests and believe that, if the bush is logged properly, there will be little evidence of intrusion. Others claim there is 'a living for a lifetime' if selective logging systems are used. Clearfelling means that an ecosystem that has formed over centuries 'is gone in a minute and there is no future for anybody'.

latifola), which were blocking, not filtering or cleaning, the waterways were removed to be replaced with native grasses, including poas and the rush *Juncus pallidus*. Where each willow was removed from the banks of the creek, a 'riffle'—a local word meaning weir or small wall—was installed, resulting in wonderful waterfalls, while also preventing erosion in times of heavy rainfall. These measures have served to protect endangered frogs. Native birds, including the small quail, shrike thrush and Tasmanian native hen have returned; these were almost non-existent when the Hawkins arrived at Bentley and can now, with the protective grass cover, move between the lakes and woodland.

The native iris—once used by the Aboriginal people for making baskets—has returned, as well as three species of eucalypt on the banks of the creek.

A feature of the gardens and paddocks is a series of sculptures in local dolerite by German artist Helmut Schwabe. These works have been carefully placed in an axis from the front lawn, through the conservatory in the centre of the house, to the lake and beyond to Mount Roland to the north-west, and are intended to bring the mountains down to the lake. They are not named, as the Hawkins like to feel they are part of the landscape. There are five low, flat stones, their polished surfaces reflecting the sun; placed on the front lawn, they don't interfere with the sweep of the wall. Beyond the house upright stones, which create an eclipse as the sun sinks, lead to the stepping stones across to the island which, one might imagine, continue beneath the lake, emerging on the other side.

The Chudleigh Valley is an area of extraordinary beauty, its pristine alpine valleys providing the entrance to mountains such as Mother Cumming's Peak and the nearby, but more accessible and busier Cradle Mountain. The controversy over the logging of forests of high conservation value often takes centre stage in this otherwise peaceful place, however.

It may not be long before the region's native forests are replaced with a monoculture of Tasmanian blue gum, and the physical and cultural geography of this beautiful place is changed forever.

Opposite: The Platypus Karst is close to Bentley, located in a precious wet sclerophyll forest of *Eucalyptus obliqua*, *E. viminalis*, white-top (*E. delegatensis*) and the fine-barked varnish wattle, *Acacia verniciflua*. Among many such limestone caves or sink-holes in northern Tasmania, this karst—or cave—is protected by its owner for its flora and fauna and the crucial part it plays in the subterranean water and ecosystem of the area. An understorey of stinkwood (*Zieria arborescens*) and musk daisy-bush (*Olearia argophylla*), a beautiful timber for cabinet-making, plays host to mosses and the bat's wing fern and with the ancient native tree ferns (*Dicksonia antarctica*) send their roots into the limestone.

LIMESTONE KARSTS

Limestone karsts, with their important subterranean drainage and aquifer characteristics, lie beneath some 277 000 hectares, or 4.4 per cent, of Tasmania. Three hundred areas are thought to have karst bedrock, although detailed studies have been carried out at just a few sites. The presence of subterranean water and its drainage through karst systems has crucial implications for land management, in particular in relation to the herbicides and pesticides used in logging practices. Logging itself has negative impacts upon karst systems, among them flooding and silting.

Garden

New South Wales

South of my days' circle, part of my blood's country,
rises that tableland, high delicate outline
of bony slopes wincing under the winter,
low trees blue-leaved and olive, outcropping granite—
clean, lean, hungry country ...

JUDITH WRIGHT, 'SOUTH OF MY DAYS', VERSE 1, LINES 1–5

The region known as the New South Wales South-West Slopes and Plains is as quintessentially antipodean as you will find. In January majestic yellow box bend contorted limbs over aestivating golden grasses; casuarinas hug the banks of slow-moving creeks and sway in a gentle breeze. Granite boulders dot the shimmering hillsides. A flash of green and yellow darting through the air tells you that this is red-rumped parrot country. This is Australia.

A historic homestead sits in this landscape, at the centre of a cattle and polo property. The gardens reconstructed here towards the end of the twentieth century pay homage to the Anglo-Saxon immigrants who settled this ancient continent, while acknowledging the rugged environment in which they rest. In the late 1980s, the landscape designer Vladimir Sitta (b. 1954) was called in by the owners and given a free hand. He has created a series of green spaces enclosed by hedges and walls and connected by paths of local granite—a garden that is supremely restful, but also exciting and full of surprise.

Opposite: The Birch Walk is underplanted with a restricted palette of *Helleborus* × *hybridus*, along with daffodils, which bloom through August and September. Earlier plantings of massed ivy proved too aggressive.

A long, gently winding drive lined with spotted gum (*Eucalyptus maculata*) leads you past post-and-rail fences—blackened in the Australian country way with creosote—which edge yellow-dry paddocks.

A tall cypress hedge surrounds and protects the terraced lawns in front of the homestead, which was built as a single storey in 1883 and to which a second level was added in 1903. Draped in an ancient wisteria and shaded by two liquidambars—which cope well with summer heat that often reaches 40 degrees Celsius—the house now affords views over the garden and landscape beyond. The lawn that rolls out from the wide front verandahs is a mix of tall fescue and rye, highlighted by three squares of bent that take on a blue sheen in winter. Cherries (*Prunus serrulata* 'Kanzan') create moving shadows on this grassed terrace.

Wide granite steps lead to a lower lawn terrace, shaded by magnolias, a ginkgo and a century-old pepper tree (*Schinus molle* var. *areira*), now twisted with age into a sculptural form. A path leads across this lawn to the 'Green Cathedral', created from Italian alders that are planted on a slope, leaning in towards a central void. Grass in this area is cut to create a

Opposite, top: The summer landscape of South-West Slopes and Plains, New South Wales. *Opposite, centre*: Like much of Australia, this country was once cleared for grazing. Now indigenous yellow box (*Eucalyptus melliodora*) and Blakely's red gum (*E. blakelyi*) shade the paddocks again. *Opposite, bottom*: The homestead was built in 1883 for a local pastoralist family. *Top, left*: The top terrace: a hedge of *Escallonia bifida* backs a border of agapanthus, which provides colour throughout summer. *Top, centre*: The lower lawn is the setting for 'Three Spheres', a work in bronze by Raphael Benazzi. *Top, right*: A driveway of spotted gum (*Eucalyptus maculata*) leads into the property. *Above*: Silver birch, *Betula pendula*.

Top, left: The vegetable garden is punctuated by standard bay trees and tripods of beans. Top, centre: Water lilies. Top, right: A woodland of the indigenous river she-oak (*Casuarina cunninghamiana*) leads to the native lily pond. **Above:** The Green Cathedral, created from Italian alder (*Alnus cordata*), is entered by a spiral of granite steps. **Opposite, top:** The White Garden on the upper level to the Pool Garden. **Opposite, bottom:** A retaining wall in the Pool Garden is softened with a covering of Virginia creeper (*Parthenocissus quinquefolia*) and curtains of Chinese star jasmine (*Trachelospermum jasminoides*) provide scent each spring. The Fog Folly is an extraordinary creation from which clouds of cool mist billow at the flick of a switch.

different texture: it is the water-wise kikuyu and is oversown with rye to ensure the area remains green through winter frosts.

A walk of silver birch, underplanted with hellebores, leads to the Pool Garden and on to one of the most exciting of several virtuoso water features that Sitta has installed throughout the garden. Dubbed 'Fog Folly', it hides the pool equipment with clouds of mist, which rise, cool against a clear blue sky, when triggered by the flick of a switch.

Above, on a higher level reached by a sweep of granite edged in clipped orbs of hebe, a swath of smooth-trunked lemon-scented gums (*Corymbia citriodora*) reminds you once more that you are, indeed, in Australia.

THE DESIGNER
IN THE GARDEN

The relationship between garden designer and client is one that is layered with meaning: there is commitment, experience, dedication, passion and, occasionally, the beginnings of a life-long friendship. The challenge for the designer must lie in comprehending the client's dreams and aspirations, and translating them into a form that is achievable and sustainable. The personal tastes of the owner are central to the imagined design, as are considerations about the ways in which the garden will be used. For the client, the goal must be the gift of a garden that has the stamp of the designer, but the personality of the owner, upon it.

VILLA
Valmarana
AI
Nani

[Vicenza is] ... a city of not very large
circumference, but full of noble intellects.

ITALIAN ARCHITECT ANDREA PALLADIO (1508–1580)

When contemplating northern Italy, you may think first of Milan and its association with fashion, or of Venice and romance, or of the Italian Lakes and scenery that leaves you gasping at its beauty. You should also think of Vicenza, a city of restrained and elegant architecture, a living tribute to one of the greatest of all architects, Andrea Palladio.

Vicenza lies in the Veneto region, protected on three sides by the Berici Hills and cooled by tributaries of the Brenta River. The town is only a couple of hours west of the glittering Italian Lakes and not far from Venice to the east, shimmering in the milky, pink light of the Adriatic.

The city became home to Palladio, born in nearby Padua, after he arrived there as a young stonecutter. His patron was the nobleman Giangiorgio Trissino, for whom he created several grand town and country residences. Palladio's stripped-down buildings of perfect proportions have influenced architecture the world over: his ideals were taken to England by Lord Burlington in the early eighteenth century and copied by Thomas Jefferson for his beloved home, Monticello, and for the University of Virginia at Charlottesville (*see* pages 129–31). Vicenza became a mecca for the English

Opposite: Valmarana's Pallazina overlooks a wide terrace with a circular bed of *Rosa* 'Mutabilis' encased in box and another of seasonal displays: in spring, tulips, and in summer, canna lilies. The southern side of the front terrace sports a collection of the full-flowered David Austin roses.

Above: This elegant pagoda is set in a woodland of ancient oaks and elms. *Opposite, top*: Paths of crushed gravel lead to a niche backed with black-green hedges of common yew, *Taxus baccata*. *Opposite, bottom left*: Family and guests take regular *pasegiata* under the cool canopy created by *allées* of ancient hornbeam, *Carpinus betulus*. *Opposite, bottom right*: A delicate wrought iron gate at Villa Valmarana ai Nani is set into a robust hedge of European hornbeam, *Carpinus betulus*.

who, on their Grand Tour of the Continent, rested there to study the refined perfection of Palladio's work. Today the city remains a monument to the architect, with its Teatro Olimpico, palaces and villas, which have been classified among the UNESCO World Heritage sites.

Among the two dozen villas that reflect the ideals of Palladio—built in and around Vicenza for noble families of the region and wealthy Venetians escaping the city's oppressive summer heat—is the Villa Valmarana ai Nani. It was constructed in two stages: the first in 1665 for a judge and the second after it was bought by Giustino Valmarana in 1720. Valmarana called in the leading architect and garden designer Francesco Muttoni (1667–1747), a devotee of the work of Palladio and its 'neo-interpretation' in the eighteenth century.

The villa, which stands on an expansive, south-facing terrace overlooking formal Italianate gardens, remains occupied by the Valmarana family today. Among its treasures are the frescoed ceilings and walls, executed by Giambattista (or Giovanni) Tiepolo and his son Giandomenico, who were engaged by Valmarana in 1757. The villa's main building, the Palazzina, houses dazzling frescoes depicting classical Greek themes—from Dido to Diana—painted by Tiepolo Snr. A guest house or *foresteria* (in which many of the works were painted by his son) and the stables were also spared the devastation of World War II.

On one side the terrace, which is edged in low walls of local stone, affords wonderful views over La Valetta di Silensio, 'The Little Valley of Silence'. The villa is protected on the other side of the property by 4-metre-high stone walls, now decorated with the seventeen dwarfs, after which Valmarana is named—*ai nani*. Designed by Giandomenico Tiepolo—in the same year the villa was decorated with its glorious frescoes—and created by Francesco Uliaco, these somewhat disgruntled-looking dwarfs were originally placed throughout the gardens in the fashion of the time.

According to Contessa Carolina Valmarana, the villa is tied to the legend of a dwarf princess, whose father protected her with a contingent of dwarfs. One day, when a handsome prince arrived, the princess jumped off the wall in desperation, to her demise; in their grief the dwarfs turned to stone.

The half-hectare front garden of the Pallazina is dominated by roses. A circular, box-edged bed—scaled up to suit the dimensions of the terrace—houses the old China, butterfly-like rose 'Mutabilis', which opens in yellows and pinks and deepens to a crimson.

Top, left: A pink shrub rose, the very remontant 'Calliope', was bred in 1985 by Barni Roses, a large rose grower located at Pistoa, between the cities of Florence and Lucca. 'Calliope', with its frilled edges, resembles that most elegant of modern climbers 'Madame Grégoire Staechelin' which, however, only blooms once, in late spring. *Top, centre left*: The David Austin–bred rose 'Graham Thomas'. *Top, centre right*: R. 'Dolce Luna'. *Top, right*: R. 'Notturno'. *Bottom*: The rear terrace, protected by tall hedges of cypress, is decorated with urns planted with citrus. Deep beds of hydrangea flower through summer in the protective shadow of the house.

ROSA 'MUTABILIS'

It is thought that *Rosa* 'Mutabilis' was given to the wider horticultural world by the Swiss botanist Henri Correvon, who obtained it from Isola Madre— where it still grows in a 2-metre-high hedge—after its introduction from China in the late nineteenth century.

The David Austins—those voluptuous roses bred in England for repeat-flowering, disease resistance, perfume and their blowsy, old-fashioned form—fill wide borders along the length of the terrace. The golden-flowered 'Graham Thomas', in honour of the celebrated English rosarian Graham Stuart Thomas; 'Golden Celebration'; the gorgeous, frothy 'Eglantyne', which opens a blush pink in late spring and blooms apricot in autumn; the apricot 'Evelyn'; and the pink 'Mary Rose' all bloom continuously here.

Valmarana houses a collection of roses bred by the Italian firm Rose Barni, which includes the pink *Rosa* 'Calliope', introduced in 1985, and the very scented lilac-to-pink 'Dolce Luna', introduced in 1999. The French-bred climber 'Pierre de Ronsard' (named after the favourite poet of Charles IX of France, Queen Elizabeth I of England, and the abbot of a priory in Brittany) blooms in coconut-ice colours, hoisting itself over the boundary wall.

Behind the Pallazina, terraces are decorated, in the traditional way, with urns filled with citrus. A series of stone comedic figures, including statues of courtiers from *commedia dell'arte* (a form of improvisational theatre)—in the fashion of the eighteenth century and which are idiosyncratic of these great gardens of the Veneto region—rest among ancient hornbeams and oaks.

Naumkeag

*The truth is I am in love with the place—
the climate, scenery, life & all.*

**EDITH WHARTON TO HER FRIEND THE ARCHITECT OGDEN CODMAN JNR WITH
WHOM SHE CO-AUTHORED *THE DECORATION OF HOUSES* IN 1897**

Edith Wharton, aunt to the landscaper Beatrix Jones Farrand (*see* pages 61–5), adored the Berkshires, a calm, mountainous area of picturesque villages a few hours' drive from either Boston or New York. Like generations of other artists, Wharton was inspired by the clear air and rustic atmosphere of the region, eschewing the more flamboyant tone of the privileged retreat of glittering Newport, Rhode Island, and the coastal Maine villages where her niece was creating a collection of outstanding gardens.

The Berkshires are also the site, however, of many grand gardens built during America's so-called Gilded Age, an era that flourished during the latter half of the nineteenth and early decades of the twentieth centuries. The region provided refuge for east-coast industrial and banking families, who spent late summer and early autumn in leisurely days picnicking, riding, and playing tennis and the new game of golf.

Naumkeag, a Native American word meaning 'Haven of Peace', was commissioned from the architectural firm of McKim, Mead & White by the prominent New York barrister and diplomat Joseph Choate and his

Opposite: Naumkeag's acclaimed Blue Steps, designed by Fletcher Steele in 1939, lead from the house to Mabel Choate's picking garden at the base of the steep slope down which the garden is arranged. Writing of this ambitious design, Choate recalled, 'I told Mr Steele he must make me some steps that would be both convenient and easy. Little did I realise what I was in for ...' The steps, with their strident Art Deco railings, also cleverly disguise structures that channelled water from the top of the garden to its base.

artist wife, and was completed in 1886. On the outskirts of the charming village of Stock-bridge, the house is built in the articulated shingle 'cottage' style popular at the time, on the upper level of the property that covers more than 20 sloping hectares.

The gardens that you see today are the work of Mabel Choate, who inherited Naumkeag after the death of her parents. Mabel worked with the dashing Boston landscape architect Fletcher Steele (1885–1971), who had trained with the distinguished Frederick Law Olmsted (1822–1903); between 1926 and 1956, they created a series of 'garden rooms' influenced by a recent tour of Californian gardens, and based on several impressive terraces.

There are a peony terrace, Chinese gardens—built to house treasures collected during journeys to the Far East and accessed by an elegant moon gate—a serpentine rose walk and a cutting garden. Fletcher Steele added significant structural elements, including a topiary walk, to define space and provide perspective.

Opposite, top: The writer Edith Wharton (1862–1937) bought land in the heart of the Berkshires, Massachusetts, to escape what she described as 'the vapid watering place amusements in which days are wasted' of east coast summer resorts. Her lavishly decorated house, The Mount—a 42-room mansion, was built with the proceeds of her novels. Wharton took up residence there in 1902 and entertained a stream of illustrious visitors, including Henry James. *Opposite, bottom:* Naumkeag, set on its steep site. *Top, left to right:* Mabel Choate adored peonies. *Above:* Mabel Choate was influenced by her travels in the East.

Above: The serpentine rose walk at Naumkeag was designed in 1953 by Fletcher Steele to be viewed from Mable Choate's bedroom. Paths of pink marble gravel wind through sixteen beds of floribunda roses, like ribbons rolled out across the grass. The house commands arresting views across wild meadows of the outer garden and the Berkshire Hills. *Opposite:* The Afternoon Garden, an enclosed terrace extending from the western side of the house, was created by Fletcher Steele in 1926 as an outdoor room for summer entertaining. The Venetian influence is evident in the parterre that surrounds the shallow, black glass pool.

Important to the atmosphere of the gardens is the pastoral element of their design, reflecting the idyllic nature of this holiday retreat. To the west of the house are fields for grazing cattle and a picturesque barn, plus pig and chicken houses and a large vegetable garden. Fletcher Steele and his client supervised the lopping of some woodland in the distance so that they would reflect the silhouette of Bear Mountain on the horizon.

In 1958 Mabel Choate bequeathed Naumkeag to the Trustees of Reservations, an organisation devoted to the preservation of important properties in Massachusetts. The house and gardens have been maintained as client and designer created them.

THE EMERALD NECKLACE

In North America's Boston there are 3 kilometres of linked green spaces designed by the nineteenth-century landscape architect Frederick Law Olmsted (1822–1903) called the Emerald Necklace. They were created as an essential lung for the city and underwent restoration in the late 1980s. Olmsted regarded parks as civilising influences in society, as a vehicle for human beings to escape turmoil into a serene environment and engage with vistas, trees and green space. The pre-eminent American landscaper of his time, and now often referred to as the 'Father of American Landscape Architecture', Olmsted is perhaps best known for New York's Central Park. He was also responsible for Prospect Park in Brooklyn, and the park systems in Boston and Buffalo; was instrumental in the preservation of Yosemite and Niagara Falls as national parks; and was the designer of Riverside, Illinois, the first planned suburb.

Boston's Emerald Necklace incorporates six parks totalling more than 500 hectares, and embraces several lakes and waterways, the Arnold Arboretum and more than a kilometre of community gardens, which flourish in the shadow of the city skyscrapers and provide a great deal more than peas and beans.

Spring is the perfect time to take a walking tour through south Boston and the Emerald Necklace. Within the series of linked green spaces, Olmsted Park houses a collection of oaks, maples, willows and liquidambars and vibrant birdlife. Beyond it a stroll through an extensive rose garden leads to the community gardens. Some are smart; some a hotchpotch of flowers, fruit and vegetables. Many seem to be a home away from home for their owners: chairs and umbrellas sit ready for when the garden work is done.

Stevens-Coolidge Place

Let Every house be placed if the Person pleases in the middle of its plot so that there may be ground on each side for Gardens or Orchards, or fields, so that it may be a green Country Town ... and will always be wholesome.

WILLIAM PENN (1644–1718), ENGLISH QUAKER AND FOUNDER OF PENNSYLVANIA, USA, INSTRUCTING HIS COMMISSIONERS WHEN PLANNING THE CITY OF PHILADELPHIA IN 1861

Stevens-Coolidge Place is a perfectly preserved example of the American Colonial Revival Movement, about an hour's drive north of Boston, in the small town of North Andover, Massachusetts. Today maintained by the Trustees for Reservations, a heritage organisation established in 1891, the property—formerly known as Ashdale Farm—was farmed for six generations by descendents of the area's first settlers, John and Elizabeth Stevens, who arrived from England in the 1640s.

John and Elizabeth's direct descendant Helen Stevens married the diplomat John Gardner Coolidge—related to Thomas Jefferson and a nephew of the Boston collector and philanthropist Isabella Stewart Gardner—in 1909. They engaged the pre-eminent Colonial Revival architect Joseph Everett Chandler (*see page 95*)—who had also worked on many of Boston's colonial landmarks—to remodel their summer holiday home between 1914 and 1918. Chandler also reconstructed much of the 3-hectare garden, and its surrounding landscape, to demonstrate both the formality of the French chateau garden and the romanticism of the English country garden, referring—we might imagine—to William Robinson and Gertrude Jekyll in his design.

The property reflected the aspirations of an era that sought an idealised, pre-industrial state typified by the country retreat. The Colonial Revival Movement emphasised the development of the decorative disciplines, including architecture and gardening; it was a domestic style in

Opposite: The restored Colonial Revival house overlooks the detailed, double, perennial borders which burst with clouds of *Crambe cordifolia* complemented by blue-flowered campanulas, lavenders, pink and white peonies and clematis. At the end of the border, the formal garden gives way to a meadow.

which nostalgia for a more innocent, pre-industrial era was central—similar in its ethos to England's Arts and Crafts Movement.

The property became a showcase for the Coolidges' collections bought while posted in Peking and Paris: Asian treasures (including Chinese porcelain), American and European decorative arts and American furniture.

Joseph Chandler enhanced the gardens, highlighting the ideals of the colonial garden: formal, but not grand or ostentatious; useful as well as beautiful. They are a very personal mix of sumptuous English-style perennial borders; a formal, intimate enclosed rose garden; an elaborate French *potager*, or vegetable garden, abutting a serpentine wall; an orchard reached by wandering through a wildflower meadow; and the rustic simplicity of hayfields and woodlands.

JOSEPH EVERETT CHANDLER

A major proponent of the Colonial Revival style, the preservation architect Joseph Everett Chandler (1864–1945) was responsible for the restoration of many of Boston's seventeenth- and eighteenth-century buildings. His work was an exemplification of his belief in the importance of conserving the history of a culture and understanding it through its architecture. Among his most famous—although controversial—restorations was that of the home of silversmith and American activist Paul Revere, where Chandler removed a third storey that Revere had occupied, but which was not original.

Chandler was central to the 1910 restoration of the House of the Seven Gables in Salem, Massachusetts, returning the house to its appearance in local writer Nathaniel Hawthorne's 1851 novel of the same name. The US Department of the Interior designated the property a National Historic Landmark in April 2007, noting the importance of preserving 'a historic building in an appropriate setting in which to teach immigrants about American history and values'.

Opposite, top: The architect Joseph Everett Chandler designed the Italianate, formal walled rose garden at Stevens-Coolidge Place in 1926 as an outdoor room and a setting for garden parties. A sunken lily pond was the centrepiece of this secluded garden, which was visible from Helen Coolidge's dressing-room—this section was restored in the 1980s with roses loved by Coolidge. *Opposite centre, left to right:* Russian sage (*Perovskia atriplicifolia*); *Rosa* 'Albertine'; *R.* 'Dorothy Perkins'; *R.* 'Duchesse de Brabant'; *R.* 'The Fairy'; *R.* 'Wedding Day'. *Opposite, bottom:* A simple mown grass path wends through the wild meadow and orchard. *Above, left:* This brick serpentine wall is reminiscent of the famous serpentine wall designed by John Coolidge's ancestor, Thomas Jefferson, at the University of Virginia in Charlottesville. As well as reflecting the fashion of American colonial gardens, the wall, which was restored in 2000, serves to hide the utilitarian area of the property. *Above, right:* The French Garden. The Coolidges fell in love with the *potager*, the decorative French vegetable garden, while living in France during World War I. Original plans for the French Garden, recently discovered in the archives in the house by a postgraduate student at Radcliffe, show forty-two beds housing collections of herbs and vegetables. In the French style, annuals are mixed with vegetables, and beds are edged with decorative brickwork.

Dumbarton Oaks

The ... beauty of the formal Italian garden lies in its perspectives ... the proportions of the parts to each other and the works of art in the shape of fountain and statues which emphasize the design.

BEATRIX JONES, AGED 23, DIARY ENTRY, ON HER FIRST VISIT TO ITALIAN GARDENS, APRIL 1895

In a letter from Washington DC in July 1922, Mildred Bliss wrote to the American garden designer Beatrix Jones Farrand (1872–1959), 'Your letter and its enclosure have made us purr with contentment. You have got it exactly! In every respect, and I can't be patient until you get back here and start to realise your and our mutual dream.' Mildred was speaking of the ambitious design Farrand had created for Dumbarton Oaks, 25-odd hectares of farmland in Georgetown that she and her diplomat husband, Robert, had purchased in 1920.

Thus began a deep friendship and professional relationship between the New York–based Farrand and the heiress Mildred Bliss, seven years her junior, which was to span more than three decades. The correspondence between designer and client was littered with little intimacies: 'Angel Trix', 'Dearest Garden Twin', and 'fondest love'. Farrand returned often to work on Dumbarton Oaks until her retirement in 1951, and towards to the end of her life wrote, 'There is no place that lies dearer to my heart than Dumbarton.'

Robert and Mildred Bliss wanted a house and garden in which they could entertain: a house that would provide an appropriate canvas for

Opposite: Throughout the garden at Dumbarton Oaks, motifs and ornaments on walls and gates are heavy with symbolism, inspired by the bounty of the soil. This gate ornament was designed by landscaper Beatrix Jones Farrand in about 1922.

their collections of treasures and their library (to be made available to scholars) and a garden that would look wonderful during three seasons of the year. Robert Bliss had been a diplomat in South America and the couple had lived in Paris from 1912 to 1919. Part of an influential expatriate circle, Mildred was tirelessly involved in crucial charity work. Upon returning to the United States, Robert was keen 'to establish a solid base and a proper background ... in my own country'. He enthused that the Oaks—as the property was then called—which was less than 4 kilometres from the White House, would provide 'a country place in the city'.

The 5 hectares of formal gardens are laid out on several terraces, set in a steeply sloping site and supported by massive walls of brick and local stone connected by great flights of steps and walkways. It is easy to appreciate that the vision of both Farrand and her client was fed by the grand gardens and estates they visited on their separate travels throughout Italy and France. But while the garden pays tribute to the formality and ornamentation of the Italian Renaissance, the influence of Gertrude Jekyll (whom Farrand had first visited in England in 1895) and the Arts and Crafts Movement is evident.

The garden unfolds as a series of surprises that are enclosed by hedges and intricately designed walls and fences, which are replete with imagery and meaning; intimate spaces are connected by interrelated levels and terraces.

Farrand was fascinated by tree silhouettes. She enthused that the house was 'surrounded by magnificent oaks and placed far enough back from the adjoining streets of Georgetown to still keep a semi-rural air'. She retained most of the trees that she found on the property—

Opposite, top: The Urn Terrace at Dumbarton Oaks overlooks the formal Rose Garden and is laid out below the Beech Terrace. *Opposite, bottom*: The Federal-style house—photographed from the Star Garden, which is paved with astrological symbols—was built in 1923. This northern façade overlooks the Green Garden, a peaceful composition of stone walls, steps, paths and wide expanses of lawn, backed by a towering forest of oaks, beech and other native American trees. *Above, left*: The Orangery, its walls clad in creeping fig, *Ficus pumila*. *Above, centre*: The Fountain Terrace, at the base of the steeply sloping garden, is reached via a double flight of stone steps. *Above, right*: Mildred Bliss took great care over the details of this tribute panel, engraved in limestone, to designer Beatrix Jones Farrand. It was installed in the wall of the Green Garden in 1935.

Above: Beatrix Jones Farrand prepared a detailed planting plan for the Rose Garden which was installed in 1922, within a massive wall. *Opposite, top*: The view towards the Ellipse—a circular garden room walled with pleached hornbeam, which has replaced earlier box—is narrowed by the use of billowing box plants. These line the steps to the lower level and are clipped to create a sense of excitement and surprise. The tranquil pool of water and its central Provençal fountain are discovered suddenly, almost by chance. *Opposite, bottom*: The Italianate Pebble Pool, viewed here from above, was installed by Mildred Bliss in 1961. The pebbles are laid in the pattern of the family crest, a wheat sheaf, and offer the motto, 'As You Sow So Shall You Reap'.

mainly American oaks—to provide a unifying and strong design element throughout the garden. To these she added collections of special evergreen and deciduous trees—beech, katsura, magnolia and maple—to add structure and textural interest.

For the front garden, she advised, 'No so-called ornamental planting should be attempted ... the forms and textures should be all that is needed to give the feeling of dignity and simplicity which the lines of the building themselves demand.' Her skill lay in masterful site planning, massing of plant material to 'scale up' the design and elegant placement of ornaments.

In the lower parts of the garden, formality gives way to woodland, naturalistic plantings now so settled that they seem as if the wind and the birds have placed them there.

Farrand was acutely aware that no garden stands still and in her *Plant Book for Dumbarton Oaks* (1941), written when she was 69 years of age, she set out the details of the garden, advice on its care and maintenance, plant lists and instruction on species replacement, while retaining the integrity of the original vision.

Twelve hectares of the property were given to the National Park Service in 1940, while the gardens and the house, including its collection of pre-Columbian and Byzantine treasures and rare book and manuscript libraries, were given over to the care of Harvard University—although they remain housed at Dumbarton.

Mildred Bliss wrote of her garden, 'The onrush of spring at Dumbarton Oaks fairly leaves one breathless.' But the garden, and the collections of treasures in the house, are breathtaking at any time of the year.

New Suzhou
MUSEUM
Garden

*You would never think that a garden which will last
a thousand years could be made by the hand of man,
who lasts but a hundred.*

JI CHENG, *YUAN YE OR THE CRAFT OF GARDENS*, 1634

Today one of China's most impressive landscapes—although perhaps more austere and restrained than the traditional Chinese garden—is that surrounding the new Suzhou Museum, Jiangsu Province. Designed by Ieoh Ming (IM) Pei (b. 1917) as a gift to the city in which he spent much of his childhood, the museum uses modern technology to reflect the vernacular buildings of Suzhou: whitewashed plaster walls and grey, clay tile roofs.

In the style of the traditional architecture of the city, the museum is arranged as a series of pavilions that flow into several courtyard gardens; these, although modern, pay homage to a traditional Chinese aesthetic language. The main section of the garden is intended to mirror—in a contemporary language—the adjacent Zhuozheng Yuan or the Humble Administrator's Garden, laid out in the early sixteenth century by a retired government official on the site of an earlier temple (*see* pages 35–9).

As high walls divide the two gardens—in the classical 'hide and reveal' tradition—an expanse of water has been employed to provide a sense of continuity and connection between the two spaces. According to the writings of the garden designer, poet and painter Ji Cheng (1582 – c. 1642) in

Opposite: Rock-work in traditional Chinese gardens reflects a reverence for nature and its majestic mountain peaks. This rock mountain in Huanxiu Shanzhuang (Mountain Villa Surrounded by Elegance)—dating back to the tenth century and thought to have been constructed by the famous rockery artist Ge Yuliang—is considered to be the best lakeside rockery in Suzhou, China.

his three-volume treatise on landscape practice and theory, *Yuan Ye* or *The Craft of Gardens* (1634)—written to prevent the rising middle class from making aesthetic *faux pas* as they sought to create gardens to demonstrate their new wealth—a pool should occupy three-tenths of any garden. Each end should drift into the distance and should be spanned by bridges or edged with covered walkways to facilitate quiet contemplation. The Chinese word for landscape, *shanshui*, translates into 'mountains and water'. Rocks respresenting mountains are masculine or *yang*, while water invokes the female quality of *yin*.

A ruthlessly restricted horticultural palette is used in the gardens that surround the museum spaces. Pine, osmanthus, pomegranate and fine-leaved maple were all personally selected by IM Pei for the gardens, most from the Suzhou region. Stands of giant bamboo throughout the garden add height to the linear spaces, as well as providing dappled shade, movement, sound and texture.

Opposite: The architecture of the museum—whitewashed plaster walls and grey clay tile roofs—pays homage to traditional Chinese buildings. A single pomegranate (*Punica granatum*) forms a small tree with a rounded canopy of bright green summer leaves that turn yellow in autumn. The smooth fruit are a bright pink to red when ripe. *Above*: 'It is possible to dine without meat, but man cannot live without bamboo,' writes Su Shi, an eminent Chinese scholar of the Northern Song Period.

Above, left: The architecture of the Song Period—which lasted more than 300 years—is delicate and elegant. Close to the museum in the Shizilin or Lion Grove Garden, traditional Chinese buildings are roofed in elegant curves and decorated with symbolic motifs. *Above, centre:* Open windows are often decorated with intricate lattice work, and courtyards are shaded by maples and persimmon. *Above, right:* Following advice in *The Craft of Gardens* by Ji Cheng, the idea of 'hide and reveal' is well demonstrated in this moon gate at Shizilin or Lion Grove Garden. *Opposite:* A forest of bamboo is visible from one of the museum galleries through a picture window, reflecting the Chinese tradition of new-moon-shaped windows and gates to enhance the element of surprise, and bring a garden into built spaces.

A massive *Wisteria sinensis* forms a scented canopy to the courtyard café; it has been raised by grafting cuttings from a 500-year-old wisteria planted by a Suzhou scholar during the Ming Dynasty (1368–1644).

IM Pei spent his summers next door to the museum site in his family garden, the Shizilin or Lion Grove Garden, which was gifted to the state after 1949. Like many traditional gardens, it relies upon ornate rock-work to convey a sense of the soaring, mist-covered mountain peaks so revered by Chinese landscape painters. Rocks are crucial to the Chinese garden and, especially during the Northern Song Period (960–1127) when Chinese gardens reached their greatest height, became collectible and coveted for their idiosyncrasies.

In the museum garden, inspired by the mystical landscapes painted by Mi Fu (1051–1107), a leading artist of the Northern Song Period, IM Pei has sliced massive granite boulders into sections, creating layers of mountain ranges as an atmospheric backdrop to the long reflecting pool.

As Ji Cheng wrote in *The Craft of Gardens*, 'There is no definite way of making scenery; you know it is right when it stirs your emotions.'

Kyoto's Ancient Gardens

Design the pond with respect to its position in the land, follow its request; when you encounter a potential site, consider its atmosphere; think of the mountains and waters of living nature and reflect constantly upon such settings.

TACHIBANA-NO-TOSHITSUNA (1028–1094), *SAKUTEIKI OR NOTES ON GARDEN DESIGN*

The Japanese are masters of clarity and simplicity; understatement and refinement form the foundation of their culture and are central to their gardens, which are pared back, edited.

Garden-making is deeply embedded in Japanese culture, as is the appreciation of all things of beauty. The Japanese live, at the least symbolically, with nature: their gardens are small, idealised representations of a wider landscape. Domes of clipped azaleas may signify rolling hills or blowsy clouds, rocks can represent islands or animals, and pebbles are raked into patterns to acknowledge the daily changes in the weather. While a restricted palette of plant species contributes so much to the peace and serenity of the Japanese garden, attention to detail is also paramount.

The underlying principles of Japanese garden design derive from the observation of nature. A garden may be the literal interpretation, in miniature, of a landscape or a symbolic recreation of it through the placement of just a few rocks; for example, an allegorical journey from the mountains to the sea.

Opposite: Katsura Rikyu, completed in the Edo Period (1603–1867), was designed to lead guests on a journey, often across beautiful bridges, and along paths that wound around lakes and over low hills. By night, guests were escorted by moonlight or stone lanterns.

Inspired by the themes of Buddhism—which arrived in Japan from China in the fifth century—and which honours the balance between nature and humanity, garden-making was popular first with emperors and members of the imperial household. The powerful warlords, or shoguns, also revered garden-making as a symbol of the educated and cultivated and as a creative release from politics and war.

Throughout his life Shiro Nakane (b. 1952), one of Japan's foremost landscapers, has been acutely aware of the country's most revered and respected gardens. The son of Kinsaku Nakane, who restored many of the country's greatest gardens after the deprivations of World War II, Shiro Nakane grew up in the ancient Japanese capital of Kyoto, amid the post-war restoration of the city's treasured temples, shrines and gardens.

His personal library is the repository of the pictorial records of the rebuilding of these great gardens, sites now well known to garden lovers around the world: the Katsura and Shugakuin Imperial Gardens, the Gold and Silver Pavilions and the revered Moss Garden—sites that were neglected during World War II when survival took precedence.

The different characteristics of the Japanese garden—often painted with such a light hand that they are difficult to articulate—are influenced by the principles set out at the end of the eleventh century in *Sakuteiki*, one of the world's earliest manuals of garden design.

Opposite, top and bottom: The greatest example of the Japanese stroll garden is found at the imperial garden, Katsura Rikyu, or Katsura Imperial Villa. Set on the Katsura River to the west of Kyoto, this garden is a sublime example of the ideal of *kirei sabi*, or refined beauty through rustic simplicity. Created from about 1610 by Prince Toshihito (1571–1629)—the adopted son of Toyotomo Hideyoshi (1536–1598), the second of three warlords who united Japan in the late sixteenth century—the villa became a haven for artists, writers and garden-lovers. *Above, left to right:* Chaenomeles speciosa 'Toyo Nishiki'; *Pinus thunbergii*; *Pieris japonica*.

And Shiro Nakane, who creates Japanese gardens throughout the world, adds three essential elements: the stone lantern, water basin and pine tree, often *Pinus mugu*. The pine tree has been a feature since the eleventh century, but the water basin and stone lantern were used only from the sixteenth century.

The plant list employed in Japanese gardens is not extensive: judicious use of a restricted palette contributes to the peaceful atmosphere so central to Japanese gardens. Nowhere is the value of green more evident than in Japanese gardens.

But, contrary to popular belief, flowers are important in Japanese gardens, says Shiro Nakane, as they reflect the changing of the seasons. Early spring throughout Japan will find the hillsides covered in flowering *sakura* or cherry blossom—revered as central to ideas of elegance, delicacy and the melancholy of fleeting beauty—and azaleas about to bloom in bright hues of cerise, purple and pink.

Two species of pine are most often used in Japanese landscaping and signify endurance: the Japanese black pine (*Pinus thunbergii*) and red pine (*Pinus densiflora*), which may be shaped over decades to create layers of elegant, horizontal limbs that drape long needles. The five-leaved pine (*Pinus parvifolia*) is also used, along with the slow-growing Buddhist

THE DESIGNER IN THE GARDEN

pine (*Podocarpus macrophyllus*), which may be pruned into clouds. Shapes convey geography along with mood: a stunted pine may convey a cold alpine meadow, while a stunted tree may signify a windswept coastal scene.

Imagine the outstretched arms and fine, filigreed leaves of a Japanese weeping maple reflected in still water; the endemic *Osmanthus fragrans*, gardenias and daphne, greatly prized for their scent; or the revered *Pieris japonica*, flowering in spring with cascades of white bells against a carpet of emerald-green moss.

Ground covers include the prostrate juniper (*Juniperus procumbins*), which may be backed with a swath of prehistoric-looking cycads. Winding paths, set with stepping stones carefully placed to temper the pace of a journey, are softened with kidney weed (*Dichondra micrantha*). Paths that flank a lake may be edged with small-leaved Korean box (*Buxus macrophylla* var. *koreana*), with dwarf bamboo or sasa grass (*Pleioblastus pygmaeus*), or mondo grass.

Several other elements contribute to the success of the Japanese garden. Scale is important in the creation of a restful garden, and a balance of one-third active—that is, planted—space and two-thirds passive—unplanted—is often considered optimum to engender a sense of calm. Then comes the relationship of the garden to its environment: borrowed scenery or *shakkei*—perhaps trees in the background in a neighbouring garden or distant mountains—will make the garden appear larger than it is.

Japanese gardens fall into different categories, although several styles might be embodied in a single garden. Stroll gardens—restrained, quiet and tasteful—were often created by the ruling elite as personal pleasure grounds, while tea gardens were incorporated into the grounds of temples and embodied ideals of discipline.

Dry gardens or dry landscapes—*kare sansui*—are derived from a Zen Buddhist focus on meditation, the path to self-awareness. Temple gardens were intended to be more striking, many built by shoguns as a display of wealth and power.

Along with a minimalist respect, which eschews waste, Shiro Nakane emphasises that history and time are factors crucial to the unique nature of the Japanese garden: the national aesthetic dictates that Japan should remain steady until everything is covered in moss. Long tradition is important. Japan does not change for change's sake.

Opposite: Austere stone lanterns traditionally lit the way for visitors—here, in Shugakuin. *Above, left:* The Tea Ceremony Garden, Sento Gosho, or Retired Emperor's Villa, was created by the retired Emperor Go-Mizunoo, Prince Toshitada's uncle, in the imperial compound in Kyoto's centre. The garden and its palace were designed in collaboration with Kobori Enshu (1579–1647), a feudal lord who became influential in all aspects of Japanese cultural life, including garden design. Rustic pavilions at the water's edge, inspired by Chinese gardens, included viewing platforms and covered walkways. *Above, right:* Wood-and-earth bridges, some covered in moss, ease the way for visitors as they descend from a 'mountain' path to this peaceful scene.

The
POLITICIANS' GARDENS

Even, or perhaps especially, those who bear the weight of a nation on their shoulders rely upon simple pleasures to ensure their sanity and health. Artistic interests that feed the spirit have been pursued by many of the politicians who have left the greatest marks on history. Garden-making is one of those arts.

Jichang Yuan

(THE DELIGHT-CONVEYING GARDEN)

*The wise take pleasure in water, and the
kind find happiness in a mountain.*

**CONFUCIUS (551–479 BC), CHINESE PHILOSOPHER
AND TEACHER OF PRINCIPLES OF CONDUCT**

The bustling city of Wuxi lies on the shores of Lake Taihu, just a little
north-west of Suzhou in the Jiangsu Province. Nestled in woodlands at
the base of the hills on the western edge of the city is a peaceful retreat,
the aptly-named Jichang Yuan or the Delight-Conveying Garden—sometimes translated as the Garden for Ease of Mind. Built on the site of an
earlier monastery by Qin Jin, an important official in the court of Emperor
Zhengde (1491–1521) during the Ming Dynasty, the garden was owned by
the Qin family, which had become powerful during the Southern Song
Dynasty (1127–1279). In 1952 the family donated the garden to the state.

Jichang Yuan is now more than half a millennium in age and, although
no doubt changed over the centuries, is considered the perfect mix of
built environment and nature. Constructed into the base of the Huishan
Hill, the garden was much visited and copied by China's emperors. Several springs on the site flow into a marble pool and are said to provide the
second best water in China for tea-making. Mountains have been created

Opposite, left: The view-finding moon gate at Jichang Yuan, or the Delight-
Conveying Garden. **Left**: The Xishan Mountain and ethereal Longguang (Dragon's
Light) Pagoda in the distance are visible through the branches of a revered
400-year-old maidenhair tree, *Ginkgo biloba*.

throughout the garden to reflect the hillside on which it rests, blending the surrounding landscape with meticulous construction work.

In the manner of private gardens, which were not as expansive as imperial landscapes, great attention was paid to architectural details. Several small courtyard gardens are scattered throughout the garden, each paved in a different decorative pattern. The most important section of the garden is perhaps the Jinghuiqi Pool, a lake with pavilions, covered walkways and other resting places arranged on its eastern and northern shores.

Along with other classical gardens found in today's China—either extant or restored—this garden employs a restricted palette of plants that have been celebrated by artists and writers for hundreds of years.

Pots of azaleas represent the outdoors in confined spaces, while the flat, lacy blooms of *Viburnum macrocephalum* f. *keteleeri* light up small, rockery-enclosed rooms. A 400-year-old

Opposite, top: The Jinghuiqi Pond (The Ripple of the Pooled Brocade), with its accompanying covered walkways and other resting places (including, at its centre, the View-Watching Pavilion) laid out on its eastern and northern shores. *Opposite, bottom*: Evergreens, rocks, intricately patterned paving and a view-finding moon gate: the Chinese garden vernacular. *Top, left to right*: Vignettes at Jichang Yuan highlight the importance given to architectural details in Chinese gardens. Small courtyard gardens are each paved in a different decorative pattern. *Above*: A lovely stone bridge at Jichang Yuan leads from a small enclosed space into another garden 'room'.

Top, left and right: The brilliant season-round colour of *Acer palmatum* Dissectum Atropurpureum Group graces the gardens of Jichang Yuan. ***Above, left***: *Viburnum macrocephalum* f. *keteleeri*. ***Above, centre***: Among the trees in the garden is an ancient *Ginkgo biloba*, aptly called the maidenhair tree; its rich green, feathered foliage renders coolness and tranquillity to the garden. The leaves turn butter yellow in autumn. ***Above, right***: *Codiaeum variegatum* in the Lion Grove Garden.
Opposite: The marble pool that collects the spring water at Jichang Yuan.

maidenhair tree (*Ginkgo biloba*)—that living fossil long revered in China, but only rediscovered by the West in the twentieth century—thrives in one of the several walled spaces.

Among the instructions in Ji Cheng's *Yuan Ye* or *The Craft of Gardens* (1634) is the idea of 'borrowed scenery' or *jie jing*—a distant view of mountain peaks or the trees in a neighbour's garden is greatly valued. At Jichang Yuan, the five-storeyed Longguang (Dragon's Light) Pagoda towers over the garden.

Ji Cheng also advised upon the importance of walls, which can divide space, screen, hide, enclose and create privacy. Glimpses of secondary or distant views can be framed by moon gates, vase-shaped doorways or crescent windows. Walls, often whitewashed or rubbed with other colours, serve as a background or foil, or accentuate or frame more detailed arrangements of plants and rocks.

Mount Vernon

ESTATE

I can truly say I had rather be at home at Mount Vernon with a friend or two about me, than to be attended at the seat of government by the officers of State and the representatives of every power of Europe.

GEORGE WASHINGTON (1732–1799), FIRST PRESIDENT
OF THE UNITED STATES FROM 1789 TO 1797

Some 8 kilometres from Washington DC, and close to the historic river port of Alexandria, lies George Washington's beloved Mount Vernon Estate, open to the public since 1860. The land had been in Washington's family since 1674, when King Charles II granted 2500 hectares to John, his great-grandfather. Among his many farms and houses, Mount Vernon was the place Washington thought of as home.

After leading the colonial forces to victory in the American War of Independence (1775–1783), Washington returned in 1783 to develop Mount Vernon into a farming enterprise covering some 4000 hectares. During his eight years as the nation's first president (from 1789), he visited the estate many times to oversee the building of the house and the creation of the grounds.

In 1858, in the turbulent years before the outbreak of the Civil War (1861–1865), the house and 100 hectares of land were bought from Washington's great-great nephew by the Mount Vernon Ladies' Association. The association was founded to save the home of the nation's first

Opposite: George Washington's large estate, Mount Vernon, located on the Potomac River, typifies the style of colonial residences, and their gardens, that reflected the traditional English and Dutch seventeenth-century fashions brought by the first immigrants to the new world.

president—an early and prescient act of philanthropy. The meticulously restored mansion, greenhouses, stables, slave quarters and gardens welcome more than one million visitors annually.

Set on wide lawns that roll down to the broad, languid Potomac River, and with carefully created and maintained views over the low Maryland hills, the grand colonial house and its park and gardens were developed by Washington as an American version of an English gentleman's country seat. (Despite the war, the southern ties with England remained strong, with the south providing cotton for the Midlands' mills, and indigo for naval uniforms.) The prosperity of the southern colonies and states was founded upon agriculture—mostly tobacco-growing—and, of course, free labour.

Washington designed four separate gardens at Mount Vernon. These and the house have now been restored to follow the original plans, uncovered from archaeological digs and through details gleaned from Washington's extensive correspondence and diaries. Lovers of history, and of gardens, are fortunate that financial constraints meant little was changed by Washington's descendents after his death.

The first gardens in America, as in all frontier settlements, were designed for survival; flower gardening followed when colonists had the time and means for leisure. At Mount Vernon, the walled upper garden pays tribute to the continued pleasure gained from growing food, and from utilising the produce offered by the soil. In this enclosed garden, with its elegant seed-raising houses located in opposite corners, lavish displays of flowers were mixed with fruit trees to create an extensive pleasure and productive garden. Paths edged with English box were designed for strolling, wide enough to accommodate extravagant skirts. Gifts of botanical treasures—sent from governments, scientific institutions, collectors, friends and admirers from around the world—were planted throughout the grounds; many were also housed in the greenhouse, which was engineered to include a subsurface hot-air tunnel to sustain delicate plants, including citrus, during bitter Virginia winters.

Just beyond the bowling green, which rolls out like velvet in front of the house, lies the kitchen garden—again reflecting a colonial respect for the raising of produce. It is bordered by two elegant serpentine walks shaded by tulip trees (*Liriodendron tulipifera*), white ash and elm. Parkland stretches out to ha-ha walls—which protected the garden from cattle without obstructing the view—and on to dense woodland filled with both indigenous and exotic species. A program of cloning trees planted by Washington is underway, so that when a 'champion tree'—one that was witness to his life—is lost, it can be replaced with a duplicate.

Today Mount Vernon's farm site—with its eighteenth-century breeds of oxen, mules, horses, sheep, pigs and poultry, and crops grown in Washington's time—reflects both the colonial preoccupation with self-sufficiency and the former president's creativity and energy.

Top: Mt Vernon's decorative seed-raising houses stand at opposite corners in the walled upper garden, which housed flowers, fruit and vegetables. *Centre, left:* George Washington's account book for August 1776 noted the purchase of '450 cabbage plants', along with turnip and parsley seed—even though the colonies were in the midst of the war with Britain and the nation's attention may have been on matters other than garden-making. *Centre:* Wonderfully scented lilac, *Syringa vulgaris*. 'Removed two pretty large and full grown lilacs to the [upper] garden,' Washington wrote in his diary on 22 February 1785. *Centre, right:* Borders of hot-coloured flowers in bloom in July. *Bottom:* Outside the walled garden, the warm colours of daylilies and *Echinacea* dominate the garden beds.

Monticello

We hold these truths to be self-evident, that all men are created equal, that they are endowed by their Creator with certain unalienable Rights, that among these are Life, Liberty and the pursuit of Happiness.

THE DECLARATION OF THE THIRTEEN UNITED STATES OF AMERICA, PRESENTED TO CONGRESS 4 JULY 1776

Thomas Jefferson (1743–1826) is best known as the third president of the United States (from 1801 to 1809) and as the principal author of the Declaration of Independence. He also achieved distinction as an Enlightenment man of science and the arts (including architecture). As well, he was a landscaper, and his first love may well have been Monticello, the home and garden he created at Charlottesville, Virginia.

Jefferson started building Monticello in 1768, but remodelled it after spending several years as trade commissioner to France; the Palladian mansion was completed in time for his retirement from public life in 1809. Set amid thousands of hectares of land that Jefferson had inherited from his father at the age of fourteen, Monticello—which means 'little mountain'—rests on a high plateau that affords views over the Blue Ridge and the surrounding countryside.

Influenced by the picturesque scenes and pastoral style of the eighteenth-century English landscape school—made popular by the work of William Kent, Lancelot 'Capability' Brown and Humphry Repton (*see* pages 15–19)—and his visits to the acclaimed estates of the United Kingdom and Europe, Jefferson laid out the grounds at Monticello with wide lawns enclosed by flower borders, with fruit and vegetable gardens and extensive woodlands of native and exotic trees. He decreed, however, that restraint was paramount and commented that 'art appears too much' at the extravagant Blenheim Palace in Oxfordshire, England. Although the

Opposite: Thomas Jefferson was inspired by the work of the sixteenth-century Italian architect Andrea Palladio, when designing his beloved Monticello. Building began in 1768, and was completed in time for Jefferson's retirement from public life, in 1809.

Top: Jefferson laid out the grounds at Monticello with wide lawns enclosed by flower borders, and extensive woodlands of native and exotic trees. The Roundabout flower border—a serpentine walk, edged on each side with flowers—was planted in 1807 to encircle the west lawn. *Bottom, left*: Lavateras, which fill the flower borders that edge the serpentine walk, attract bees. *Bottom, centre and right*: There are also many species of wildflowers at Monticello, collected during the early nineteenth-century exploration of the west by Meriwether Lewis and William Clark, whom Jefferson sponsored and promoted.

wealth of the southern states was built on an agricultural economy made possible by slave labour—as was the success and beauty of his own estate—the naturalistic garden was central to Jefferson's ideals of the new liberal United States.

Located 10 kilometres from Charlottesville (where Virginia University was built from 1817 to 1826, following Jefferson's plans and inspired by the early sixteenth-century Italian architect Andrea Palladio), Monticello combines interior and outdoor spaces by the use of two wide wooden verandahs, which embrace an oval-shaped lawn.

In 1807 the Roundabout border was planted—a serpentine walk, flanked with flowers, encircling this west lawn. Jefferson wrote to the nurseryman Bernard McMahon in 1811, 'I have an extensive flower border in which I am fond of placing handsome plants or fragrant. Those of mere curiosity I do not aim at ...'

A monumental vegetable garden, 300 metres long by 30 metres wide, and a 3-hectare orchard were laid out on terraces cut into the mountainside. The vegetable garden, recreated in 1979, contained more than 250 varieties of seventy different species of vegetables, including a dozen varieties of his favourite, peas. 'I must say a word to you about the Succory [chicory] you ... were so kind to give me some of the seed,' he wrote to George Washington from Monticello in September 1795. 'I consider it one of the greatest acquisitions a farmer can have. I sowed at the same time 2 acres of Lucerne ...'

Jefferson was an inveterate record keeper; his detailed notes on the gardens, along with letters to and from friends and colleagues, were published in 1944 as *Thomas Jefferson's Garden Book*. This fascinating tome reveals that trees were a crucial part of his dream for the garden, and visitors were often given a tour of his 'pet trees', among them a massive tulip tree (*Liriodendron tulipifera*), which remains to one side of the west lawn.

The gardens at Monticello house many plants collected during the exploration of the west by Meriwether Lewis (1774–1807) and William Clark (1770–1838) who, from 1804 to 1806, led the first American overland expedition to the Pacific coast and back. There are lavateras, nicotianas and the large monkey flower (*Mimulus guttatus*), a yellow, summer-flowering perennial found in 1806; there is also the snowberry bush (*Symphoricarpos albus*), a hardy shrub that features clusters of large, snow-white berries through winter. These, and other seeds collected on this epic journey, are now marketed by the Thomas Jefferson Centre for Historic Plants, an organisation dedicated to preserving historic plant varieties and promoting Jefferson's lifelong devotion to gardening.

Jefferson wrote to the Philadelphia Museum director Charles Willson Peale, 'if heaven had given me choice of my position and calling, it should have been on a rich spot of earth, well watered. No occupation is so delightful to me as the culture of the earth.'

The Monticello gardens fell into disrepair after Jefferson's death, but were restored by the Garden Club of Virginia between 1939 and 1941, after the discovery of his sketches for the Roundabout flower border and through extensive archaeological work. This wonderful property is now on the United Nations' register of internationally significant sites.

WRITERS' GARDENS

It is interesting to consider the relationship between writers and their surroundings. In 2002, during a lecture at the Australian National University, environmental historian Tom Griffiths, drawing upon the work of political scientist Judith Brett, reflected upon the requirements for writing well: a fully imagined audience, a sense of urgency, and something interesting or important to say. And Griffiths advised that good writing happens alone. I would add that you need somewhere special to indulge that solitary pursuit: a place that soothes (just enough), excites and inspires.

Writers derive their imagination and, most importantly, their energy from various sources. One of those sources is their surroundings, whether their writing environment is a book-lined study, a café perched on a snow-covered mountain or, as Griffiths mentions, a beach shack. I would recommend the sanctuary of a garden.

Venice

AND THE GARDENS OF

Hotel Cipriani

She walks in beauty, like the night
Of cloudless climes and starry skies;
And all that's best of dark and bright
Meet in her aspect and her eyes:
Thus mellow'd to that tender light
Which heaven to gaudy day denies.

LORD BYRON, 'SHE WALKS IN BEAUTY', VERSE 1

Autumn is the best season in Venice, and winter, when the ghosts of artists long gone whisper from colonnaded squares, and the mists swirl, defying you to retrace your steps. In such restrained seasons it is easy to see why the American novelist Henry James was beguiled and why English Romantic poet Lord Byron loved the city's languid melancholy. But it's in summer that the roses cascade over walls to the water's edge. It is then that the hedges of jasmine are a mass of heady scent and when geraniums drip from window boxes.

If it's summer in Venice, it's hot. The crowds throb, the pigeons descend in flocks, and tour groups, led by guides brandishing—with varying degrees of enthusiasm—a plastic flower or fish on the end of a long stick, clog the narrow, twisting alleys. But just across the water from the Piazza San Marco, on a finger of land called the Guidecca, you can luxuriate in a more tranquil Venice.

Opposite: Arbours covered in grapevines—that remind visitors that this was once the site of a thriving vineyard—divide the rear gardens and provide welcome respite from Venice's summer heat in the grounds of Hotel Cipriani. Nearby, banks of hydrangeas thrive in the north-facing, shaded beds.

Early merchants and explorers—from Marco Polo (c. 1254 – c. 1324) to the somewhat mysterious Sebastian Cabot (c. 1484 – 1587)—brought back, among their treasures, botanical bounty from around the world: by the sixteenth century, the Guidecca had become a centre for horticultural breeding and commerce. The area was bursting with orchards and gardens of rare exotics laid out around grand palazzos. The Guidecca has long sheltered writers and philosophers who, while inspired by the ethereal fantasy that is Venice, wanted protection from its heaving centre. There are no crowds on the Guidecca but, just a few minutes away, across the canal, the pink-frosted Doges Palace shimmers, a confection in delicate filigree. The Guidecca is where you can have it all in Venice, most comfortably achieved from the revered Hotel Cipriani.

Like much in Venice, the Cipriani is shrouded in intrigue and mystery; its garden, flourishing on the site of several ancient palaces, is enveloped in history. This is where, in the sixteenth century, the Dogaressa Loredana Mocenigo Marcello, wife of Alvise Mocenigo, the CXVIII Doge, nurtured her Renaissance garden. The vineyard of 'Refosco', 'Merlot' and 'Cabernet' grapes, where Casanova is said to have courted the young novice Caterina Capretta, still thrives in the rear garden of the hotel, producing annually some 2000 bottles of 'Casanova Salso' for the hotel's cellars. And closed orders of nuns and monks still tend their vegetable gardens nearby.

Opposite, top: Dawn lights the canals of Venice, seen from the Rialto Bridge, en route to the morning fish market. *Opposite, bottom:* Here, a statue of a young sea god, Triton, riding his seahorse, emerges from a pool of water lilies. *Above, left to right:* The gardens rely for colour upon the pinks and blues of hydrangeas, lavenders, climbing roses and ivy-leaved geraniums, which tumble into the canal.

Above: The vineyard of 'Refosco', 'Merlot' and 'Cabernet' grapes, where Casanova is said to have courted the young novice Caterina Capretta, still thrives in the rear garden of Hotel Cipriani. **Opposite:** The Doges Palace and St Mark's Square beckon, a safe distance from the Guidecca, across the Grand Canal.

At the landing stage to the Cipriani, a statue of the young sea god Triton astride his seahorse emerges from a pool of water lilies. Seasonal displays of annuals surround the pool: in some months clouds of white shasta daisies billow, while in mid June it might be New Guinea Hybrid impatiens, flowering a deep pink from rosettes of thick black leaves.

Ivy-leaved geraniums (*Pelargonium* 'Parisienne') cascade from urns along the sea wall. The cerise, almost-single modern rose 'Clair Matin' romps up an ancient pine, emerging from a bed of English lavender (*Lavandula angustifolia*), flowering indigo through the shimmering summer.

The stone pine (*Pinus pinea*), which provides the vernacular to so much of the Italian landscape, grows in this garden also, gnarled and bent with age and from the winds that blow in from the Adriatic. A pergola of wisteria leads into the hotel and through to the rear garden, which is dissected by two cool tunnels covered in grapevines, bordered on one side by tall banks of a rich pink *Hydrangea macrophylla*.

A wide lawn, its centrepiece the maple *Acer platanoides* 'Crimson King'—with its crimson summer foliage that turns to gold and red in autumn—makes way for a narrow passage that leads to the hotel's casual restaurant Cips, hovering over the canal. A high wall is clothed in Chinese star jasmine, broken into panels by the iconic Italian cypress, *Cupressus sempervirens*.

In *Il Fuoco*, a glorification of Venice, the writer Gabriele d'Annunzio (1863–1938), wrote of the Guidecca, 'Everywhere orchards ... the most beautiful in the world, a Paradise on Earth ... dedicated to poetry, music and love.' Casanova would have agreed.

Sissinghurst

For no new flowers shall be born
Save hellebore on Christmas morn,
And bare gold jasmine on the wall,
And violets, and soon the small
Blue netted iris, like a cry
Startling the sloth of February.

VITA SACKVILLE-WEST, *THE LAND,* **LINES 19–24**

There have been more words written about Sissinghurst than possibly any other garden in the world. Photographed, visited, eulogised and much copied, Sissinghurst is arguably the world's most influential garden.

Located in the English county of Kent, this garden of some 8 hectares was created by the writer Vita Sackville-West (1892–1962) and her husband, Harold Nicolson (1886–1968), a diplomat and keen architect. A neglected Tudor property when purchased by them in 1930, Sissinghurst remains a mecca for garden devotees—both amateur garden-lovers and professionals—who flock here from around the world.

Sackville-West used the garden—with its walled rooms, wide borders of roses and perennials, collections of scented, exotic trees, orchards, herb gardens and meadows—as the laboratory for her writing, which included garden columns, collections of poetry, travel motifs and novels.

From 1924 almost until her death, Sackville-West wrote a weekly column for the *Evening Standard,* ensuring that she became a household name. She was passionate about her plants: of *Viburnum carlcephalum,* which

Opposite: Intimate spaces are created at Sissinghurst with mellow walls that support a variety of climbing plants: here, a doorway, framed with *Clematis montana*—and in which carmine wallflowers have made themselves at home—leads from the Tower Lawn to the Rose Garden.

blooms with heads of tiny, cream-coloured, heavenly scented flowers at the end of winter, she instructed, 'If you don't have it, get it immediately.'

The centrepiece at Sissinghurst is undoubtedly its famous White Garden, drawn in clipped box hedges to create a formal structure that is overlaid with exuberant plantings in white and creams, silvers and greys. In May, the central arbour, covered in the rampant *Rosa mulliganii* gears up to burst into white, scented blossom. The white rose 'Madame Alfred Carrière' blooms on the Priest's House, along with the white *Wisteria venusta*. The soft grey *Senecio cineraria* teams with lamb's tongue (*Stachys byzantina*), daisies and nicotiana. Tall *Lilium longiflorum* flower white, providing height, as do silver-leaved *Eryngium* and billowing clouds of the white-flowered *Crambe cordifolia*.

The formal spaces around the house, which fold out from Sackville-West's writing tower, move effortlessly to rose gardens, to the famous nuttery—underplanted with precious bulbs and lacy ferns—and on to woodland areas. A wild meadow—the seemingly simple way of marrying a designed garden with its surrounding landscape and popularised by the nineteenth-century gardener and writer William Robinson—is replete with ox-eye daisies, buttercups, corncockles, cornflowers, meadowsweet and clear-red Flanders poppies,

Opposite, top: The tower, viewed from Sissinghurst's Cottage Garden, was constructed in 1573 for a visit by Queen Elizabeth I. *Opposite, bottom*: In May, *Wisteria floribunda* 'Alba' is in full flower on the wall that runs from the moat at the base of the property to a clipped hedge in the shape of a crescent moon. Earlier Vita Sackville-West's planting of *W. venusta* flowers white in shorter racemes. *Top, left to right*: The hot colours in the Cottage Garden; the White Garden; a gate leading from the White Garden. *Above*: The intricate architectural layout of Sissinghurst is clear from the perspective of the tower. Here, the Rose Garden's central rondel, created from severely clipped yew, *Taxus baccata*.

Top: New spring growth shades a statue, standing tall on its plinth in Sissinghurst's nuttery. Lime green shuttlecock ferns (*Matteuccia struthiopteris*) and deep green trilliums contribute to its shadowy, mysterious atmosphere. *Above, left to right:* In the White Garden; the wild meadow; doorways cut into high walls covered in flowering climbers afford glimpses into unfolding garden enclosures, in the tradition of 'hide and reveal'. *Opposite:* The soft grey of *Senecio cineraria* and lamb's tongue (*Stachys byzantina*) teams with the billowing flowers of *Crambe cordifolia,* daisies, nicotiana and silver-leaved *Eryngium* in the White Garden. Tall *Lilium longiflorum* flower with roses. In May, the centre arbour of *Rosa mulliganii* gears up to burst into blossom.

swaying among tall grasses. It rolls out beneath gnarled and twisted apple trees, a wide, snaking path mown languorously through it to direct the visitor to the moat around the property's boundary.

Nigel Nicolson (1917–2004) engineered the handing over of the house and gardens to the National Trust in 1967, the year before the death of his father, so that Sissinghurst could be maintained as his parents had created it. While the garden remains an extraordinary and important historical document, essentially unchanged within the moat and walls that surround the property, it is, as he wrote, 'a living, growing, changing thing' and a vibrant work of contemporary horticulture.

Late on a summer afternoon when the crowds have gone, a golden light washes this wonderful garden with a sense that nothing exists, nor matters, outside.

La Foce

... the vast, solitary, unspoilt landscape charmed and enthralled us: to live in the shadow of that mysterious mountain, to halt the erosion of those steep hills, to transform that bare clay into fields of grain, to turn those mutilated woods green again ... that, we were sure, was the life we wanted.

IRIS ORIGO, *IMAGES AND SHADOWS*, P. 201

It is difficult to believe that the landscape in which La Foce is set was ever 'bare'; the woods ever 'mutilated'. Today, far from being 'desolate' and 'half-ruined' as writer Iris Origo adds, the gardens fold out across several terraces in a virtuoso mix of clipped restraint and colourful exuberance. Nor is the property simply the 'pretty house and gardens' that Origo commissioned from the English designer Cecil Pinsent (1884–1963) in 1926.

Italy—particularly the region around Florence—provided many attractions for English expatriates and leisured Americans in the first half of the twentieth century, between World Wars I and II. And many wanted Pinsent, who had first visited the city in 1907, to restore their houses and build their gardens. Pinsent had trained at the Royal Academy School of Architecture in London, where he was taught to eschew the naturalism of William Robinson (*see* pages 21–5) and honour formality in garden design. Over four decades Pinsent restored many rundown Italian properties, returning the glories of the Baroque, Rococo and Renaissance to the gardens; perhaps the most famous is the Villa I Tatti, designed for the art historian, dealer and collector Bernard Berenson (1865–1959). The

Opposite: La Foce's lower garden, with its octagonal pool and statue, and the sublime views over Mount Amiata. Long rectangles of box enclose bull bay magnolias, which are kept in check—in the Italian way—with careful clipping into oval-shaped trees.

Above: The Genius of the Place ... you could only be in Tuscany: a distant zig-zag of *Cupressus sempervirens* leads to La Foce.

Opposite: The garden at La Foce unfolds on several levels: viewed from the wisteria walk, Cecil Pinsent's vision is clearly seen. The first level, extensively renovated and extended by Pisent, folds out from the house. The house was built at the end of the fifteenth century as a wayside tavern and later became a hospice. 'Garden rooms' are created with clipped hedges and pergolas covered in wisteria and roses. Pots of cascading summer geraniums top stone balustrades.

Villa I Tatti and its owner were greatly admired by the American writer Edith Wharton (1862–1937), who described the 'hushed and tranquil beauty' of the Italian gardens she visited, applauding the 'contrasted tints of box and ilex and laurel, and the vivid green of the moss spreading over damp paths and ancient stonework'.

La Foce, near the Tuscan village of Chianciano Terme, close to Siena, is considered Pinsent's most important post-war garden, and with it his design career entered a new and vibrant stage.

His client, Marchesa Iris Origo, was gardening aristocracy: her mother was the American heiress Lady Sybil Cutting, who bought the fifteenth-century Medici Villa in Fiesole overlooking Florence in 1911. Iris married the Marchese Antonio Origo in 1924 and bought 1800 hectares of somewhat eroded land and its rundown buildings, with dramatic views of Mount Amiata and the valley of Orcia River.

Over fifteen years, Pinsent and his colleague, designer Geoffrey Scott (who later married Sybil Cutting), along with the Origos, created the many-layered gardens that are today superbly maintained by their daughter Benedetta. La Foce is a garden of formal enclosures, squares and rectangles, edged in low box hedges and walled with clipped evergreens—all

overlaid with exuberant plantings. The gardens unfold, on several levels, from the ochre-washed house, first to the sunken *limonaria* or citrus garden, then—by staircases of mellow stone—inexorably south, towards that extraordinary vista. Great use is made of long walkways and pergolas to lead from one compartment to the next, to create boundaries and provide a coat-hanger for climbing roses and wisteria.

Nature and art collide successfully in this part of Italy, where stands of *Cupressus sempervirens* seem to top the ridges of each languid hill, leading the eye into the distance, and the mind to ponder what lies beyond. The avenue of *Cupressus sempervirens* that meanders up the slope towards La Foce leaves you in no doubt that you are in Tuscany, and contributes enormously to the 'Genius of the Place', words used by the English essayist and poet Alexander Pope, in his letter in 1731 to his patron Lord Burlington. Wharton would applaud.

Opposite: A sweeping walkway at La Foce, shaded by wisteria and edged in lavender and roses, provides a cool walk in summer; it borders the upper rose garden and leads out towards the spectacular view over the Val d'Orcia and Mount Amiata. *Top:* The garden is arranged as a series of compartments, encased with hedges, stone walls and pergolas of wisteria and roses. Stone plinths support tubs of citrus. Tall cypress and stone pines dominate the skyline. *Above, left to right:* The Orangery; the Rose Garden; steps leading to the Rose Garden edged with peonies and lavender.

CLIPPED PERFECTION

Pruning is an activity that some gardeners face with trepidation but it is one loved by many more. Clipping, and cutting back, provides a sense of achievement and order, along with the comfortable glow of a job well done.

Clipped art—and topiary in all its fanciful forms—has many uses in garden design, and while it has fallen out of fashion over the centuries, the smaller spaces of the twenty-first-century garden have ensured its new popularity. Hedges, of course, are an integral part of most designs, whether used in a traditional way as garden dividers, or as screens, stilt hedges or low borders, or even to create parterres or mazes. They don't have to be immaculate: cloud hedges—probably inspired by the gardens of Japan, where clipped evergreens can create the world in miniature—are the answer for gardeners who don't aspire to clipped perfection.

Ryōan-ji

Oh that summer moon!
It made me go
Wandering
Round the pond all night.

BASHO, *HAIKU HARVEST*

Nestled amid forest on the lower slopes of the mountains that hug the north-western side of Kyoto, Ryōan-ji is perhaps the ultimate expression of the Japanese ideal of restraint and understatement. Home to one of the schools of the Rinzai branch of Zen Buddhism, the Ryōan-ji temple is registered as one of the Historic Monuments of Ancient Kyoto and listed as a UNESCO World Heritage site.

Once the family estate of the Fujiwaras, a leading family of the Heian Period (794–1185), the site was given to the sect after the destructive wars of the fifteenth century.

Influenced by the emphasis on the abstract expression that became popular in Japan at the beginning of the sixteenth century, this Zen Buddhist garden is a minimalist example of the *kare sansui* style of dry gardening that is central to the Japanese aesthetic.

Ryōan-ji's walled rock garden is the most photographed section of the garden and is thought to have been constructed between 1619 and 1680.

Opposite: The *kare sansui* dry garden at Ryōan-ji. The temple was built between 1500 and 1700 and represents the ethereal austerity of Zen Buddhism during the Muromachi Period (1333–1573), in marked contrast to the landscaped gardens, with their generous lakes, of the Heian Period (794–1185).

Above: Clipped perfection at Ryōan-ji: small-leaved kirin azaleas often represent a rolling sea or dewy, undulating hillsides. *Opposite:* From whichever point on the temple's wooden verandah—smoothed to an ancient patina by a million shoeless feet—the visitor views the collection of stones, one is always hidden. Cherry blossom flowers in perfect counter-point to the mellow tones of an earthen wall that surrounds this section of the gardens.

Twenty metres long by 10 metres wide, it consists of fifteen stones, arranged in five groups on raked white gravel. This has been interpreted in many different ways, but is most often thought to signify islands resting in a sea.

Rocks take on special significance in Japanese gardens. Each rock is chosen for its colour, shape and character—and with its intended garden and position in mind. They are generally less dramatic than those employed in Chinese landscaping, which reflect the rugged nature of much of that vast country's topography. In Japanese gardens the rocks might represent islands, perhaps placed in symbolic gravel 'streams'. Some are flat stepping stones; others are symbolic of fauna—for example, long-living tortoises and cranes.

The gravel on which groups of rocks rest also plays a central role in the notions the garden seeks to convey. Treated with one of a selection of rakes designed to reflect the weather, gravel will also be arranged in patterns signifying swirling eddies, raging seas or calm pools.

ZEN BUDDHISM

While the earliest forms of Buddhism arrived in Japan from China in the fifth century, Zen Buddhism, as a separate sect, arrived in the twelfth and thirteenth centuries. It promoted the ideals of honouring an awareness of all aspects of daily life, and was less esoteric than earlier forms of Buddhism, with their emphasis on meditation. Zen Buddhism placed great importance on self-discipline, austerity, restraint and simplicity, and so was embraced by the samurai class. With its emphasis on creative and artistic aspects, it was also taken up by intellectuals, including priests. Calligraphy, literature, painting and tea ceremony were all part of the disciplines practised as an avenue leading to self-understanding.

Above, left to right: *Chaenomeles japonica*; cherry blossom in bud; *Spiraea cantoniensis*.
Opposite: The expansive lake, which dates to the twelfth century and the stewardship of the Fujiwara family, is framed with more recently planted cherry blossom and in May, *Spiraea cantoniensis*.

While best known for its walled rock garden, Ryōan-ji also incorporates elements of other garden styles, from stroll garden to tea garden.

Sakuteiki or *Notes on Garden Design* is the earliest book on Japanese gardening and is thought to have been written some 1000 years ago by Tachibana-no-Toshitsuna (1028–1084), a member of the Fujiwara family. It instructs garden-makers on the placement of rocks, and the principles of borrowed landscape and 'hide and reveal' constructs. 'If there are "running away" stones, there must be "chasing stones" … If there are "leaning stones", there must be "supporting" stones. If there are "assertive" stones, there must be "yielding" stones … If there are "vertical" stones, there must be "horizontal" stones.'

The somewhat spiritual importance afforded to garden design is perhaps borne out by the fact that this treatise was originally written on two scrolls and was titled *Senzai hisho* or *Secret Discourses on Gardens*. As Tachibana-no-Toshitsuna writes, 'Gardens can be built in places where there are no ponds or streams. Such gardens are referred to as *kare sansui*.' There is, surely, no greater example than Ryōan-ji.

CLIPPED PERFECTION

Levens Hall

Oh happy garden! whose seclusion deep
Hath been so friendly to industrious hours;
And to soft slumbers, that did gently steep
Our spirits, carrying with them dreams of flowers,
And wild notes warbled among leafy bowers;

WILLIAM WORDSWORTH, 'A FAREWELL', VERSE 8, LINES 1–5

While the art of topiary has fallen out of fashion over the past few decades and, somewhat determinately, has climbed back into favour, the important visual impact of clipped plants—in whatever shape—has assured it a place in garden design. You don't have to house a menagerie of farmyard animals or jungle giants in your garden, however, to put clipped garden art to good use. Elegant pyramids, obelisks and globes, created by pruning a range of species, can be employed to great effect in large and small gardens.

If whimsy and fantasy are elements you admire in a garden, you'll love Levens Hall, surely the king of topiary gardens. Located near Kendal, in the very south of the Lake District, England, this much-photographed 2-hectare garden is anything but predictable. Laid out in 1694 by the French designer Guillaume Beaumont for Colonel James Grahme—a professional soldier and supporter of the Duke of York, who had bought

Opposite: Clipping King. At Levens Hall whimsy and fantasy combine with structure and history. Ancient yew and box are clipped into massive shapes and structures to add drama to garden compartments. Hedges hide and direct, while edges encase changing floral displays.

Above: Gravitas is created in this formal section of Levens Hall's garden by buttresses and shapes, clipped mostly from yew. Hedges in box house displays of spring tulips and changing displays of pansies and primulas.
Opposite, top and bottom: Wisteria clothes upright surfaces, in early June flowering in stunning counterpoint to the sombre yew throughout the garden.

the estate five years earlier—Levens is a garden of fanciful shapes, sophisticated parterres, mature hedges and innovative and instructive perennial borders, all set within a seventeenth-century parkland of ancient oaks.

That the gardens at Levens Hall have survived for more than three centuries is extraordinary, even more so when you consider the high level of maintenance essential for keeping them at their sharpest.

Many of the topiary shapes at Levens are massive, representative of trees and mature shrubs. There are huge cylinders, giant sharply pointed pyramids and billowing clouds. Many of the shapes have whimsical names: there is the Great Umbrella, the Jug of Morocco, the Howard Lion and the Judge's Wig. Low, well-clipped hedges house displays of annuals and spring bulbs in a more conventional way.

Topiary cones can lead the eye from one section of a garden to the next, capturing and controlling interest. Smoothly clipped shapes impart a sense of permanency to any arrangement. In a complicated border, the topiary punctuation marks serve to stop the eye—preventing detailed planting patterns and dense blocks of flowers and foliage from becoming too much

Above: At Levens Hall: hedges, punctuated with vine-covered pergolas, lead from one garden area to the next. 'I think of hedges as enclosures, and it is with hedges that you may best articulate the bony structure, the skeleton as it were, of a garden. For this a hedge should usually be close in texture, monotone in colour and sharply defined in shape,' writes Russell Page in *The Education of a Gardener*.

Opposite: Giant shapes and structures require regular clipping to invoke admiration; some have been maintained here since the late seventeenth century.

to comprehend—or manage. Topiary spheres can direct you subtly along a certain route in a garden, so cleverly that you don't know you are being manipulated. And they can add height and a sense of gravitas. At Levens Hall, the collection of topiary fulfils all these roles.

As well as using topiary to ensure constant interest and excitement, Levens Hall employs high hedges to hide, and then reveal, new themes and plantings. Structure and order are provided by such well-clipped green screens: doorways cut into hedges frame further axes, views and vignettes of the gardens.

As well as a decorative vegetable garden, a voluptuous rose garden and a parkland of mature oaks dating from 1700—on the site of a medieval deer park—Levens Hall is also the site of the first ha-ha. Put simply, a ha-ha is a ditch retained with a wall around a garden and is invisible to those looking out from the house. Particularly useful in a country garden, this construction affords a view across the landscape, without the vista being interrupted by a wire or paling fence. Created by William Kent (1685-1748)—the first of a triumvirate of great English landscapers—so that the sheep could appear to be grazing in bucolic peace within the garden picture without actually helping themselves to the precious plants, the ha-ha at Levens Hall provides the perfect conclusion to luxuriantly planted twin borders. It is, perhaps, the ultimate exemplification of the Arcadian ideal.

TOPIARY TREASURES

At Levens Hall clipping takes place throughout autumn. Shapes are created mostly from the somber yew (*Taxus baccata*)—the classic choice for topiary—along with some in golden yew to add a 'shaft of light' effect. Yew has been the hedging plant of choice for many well-known garden designers, from Thomas Mawson to Beatrix Farrand, Vita Sackville-West, Geoffrey Jellicoe, Russell Page and André Le Nôtre, as they created changes in pace and mood in the gardens they created, moving from intimate spaces into park or woodland. Yew was Gertrude Jekyll's first choice for hedges. '… no other tree is so patient of coercion … so effective as a background to the bright bloom of parterre or flower border,' she wrote in 1912 in *Gardens for Small Country Houses*. 'Its docility to shaping into wall, niche, arch and column is so complete and convenient that it comes first among growing things as a means of expression in that domain of design that lies between architecture and gardening.'

Yew is slow-growing, however, and in some climates other conifers—particularly the various *Cupressus* species—will ensure greater success. The cedar, *Thuja occidentalis* 'Smaragd'—which is an intense emerald-green in midsummer and turns bronze in winter—is also an excellent choice for topiary effects and hedging, its slow growth contributing to fine detailing and a dense finish.

Beech (*Fagus sylvatica*) is a northern hemisphere hedging classic, while in some southern hemisphere climates hornbeam (*Carpinus betulus*) is less fussy and a faster grower.

In Japan, where gardens rely upon a range of species—clipped to create nature, idealised in miniature—small-leaved azaleas might represent low hills, while banks of clipped camellias might constitute a rolling sea. Cloud-pruning of conifers provides a sense of the sky in a small space. The Australian lillypilly—there are several species of the genus *Syzigium*—takes kindly to being hedged and 'topiarised', but requires regular clipping. Drought tolerant, it is widely used for pyramids, obelisks and standards, often planted in Versailles tubs and employed in pairs.

The two boxes, English (*Buxus sempervirens*) and Japanese (*B. microphylla* var. *japonica*), look good together as a double hedge. The fast-growing Japanese box is lighter in colour; the denser, slow-growing English box can be kept cut lower. The variegated box (*Buxus sempervirens* 'Variegata'), woven into the design, provides additional detail.

Broughton Castle

About the most beautiful castle in all England ...
for sheer loveliness of the combination of water,
woods and picturesque buildings.

BRITISH MILITARY HISTORIAN SIR CHARLES OMAN ON BROUGHTON CASTLE, 1898

Once at Broughton Castle, the fourteenth-century moated and fortified manor house set in the village of Broughton in Oxfordshire, England, you want to rush to the turreted roof for a bird's-eye view of the surrounding countryside. It's from this vantage point that you can see the dreamy parkland that unfolds from the house, in increasingly natural arrangements. And it is also from here that the clever design of the exquisite Ladies' Garden, many metres below, is brought into sharp relief.

If you can discipline yourself, however, and don't head to the roof first, you will find there is a cornucopia of treats, best savoured slowly, in this garden.

Broughton Castle, the home of Lord and Lady Saye and Sele, was originally a medieval manor house, built around 1300 by Sir John de Broughton. It was surrounded by a moat and greatly enlarged in the sixteenth century; some decorations were added in the 1770s, but nothing, apart from wiring and plumbing modernisations, has been changed since.

In the seventeenth century, William, 8th Lord Saye and Sele, played a seminal part in the Civil War, and the castle was the centre of conspiracy and clandestine meetings for those opposed to Charles I. Today, however, Broughton Castle sits at the centre of peaceful, glorious gardens.

The picture-postcard village of Broughton is close to Banbury, just north of Oxford, and everything—from the pub to the sweets shop—sports the

Opposite: The wonderful Ladies' Garden is most clearly viewed from Broughton Castle's roof. Closely clipped box, in the shape of a fleur-de-lis, encases roses and perennials.

coat of arms of Saye and Sele: the Fiennes lions with the Twisleton moles. The family motto is *Fortem Posce Animum*—ask for a strong spirit. Turning at St Mary's, the village's fourteenth-century stone church, the castle is approached through a massive stable block, which ushers you across the moat and into the Tudor courtyard. This is enclosed on two sides by the stone stables, and on a third side by the parkland; the castle completes the secure square.

While the family has lived at Broughton Castle since the sixteenth century, much of the 2-hectare garden was designed by Lady Algernon Gordon Lennox, a keen gardener, in the 1890s, when a great deal of formal bedding necessitated some fourteen gardeners.

Today, virtuoso flower borders of graded colour edge the outer perimeters of the garden, from where vistas across the moat lead to sheep grazing peacefully in the lush fields. These borders are a lesson in the use of colour and foliage in garden design: in one, interwoven silvers and yellows give way to the hot reds and bronzes. Another border is home to the pale pinks and silvers of penstemons and potentillas, jazzed up with the garnet-coloured pincushion flowers of *Knautia macedonica*, the deep blue of majestic delphiniums and the white spires of tall foxgloves. The scene is softened with a backing of the frothy white blossom of *Crambe cordifolia*.

Opposite, top: Broughton Castle's long perennial border measures some 100 metres along the western section of the moat that surrounds the castle. Roses, tall-growing thalictrums, iris, foxgloves and alliums stand behind *Lychnis*, *Stachys*, *Alchemilla mollis* and species geraniums, all collapsing charmingly across the wide stone 'mowing strip'. *Opposite, bottom*: Windows cut into the mellow stone walls, adorned with roses and *Clematis* 'Vino', afford glimpses into the Ladies' Garden. *Above*: A glimpse of the moat that surrounds stately Broughton Castle—it is fed by a stream in the north-east corner and, it is thought, predates the fourteenth-century house, which forms the central hall of today's castle.

Above: American Lanning Roper, who loved things English so much that he made England his home, advised on many adjustments to the gardens and parkland at Broughton Castle, mid last century. 'Play up the beauty of the building, walls and landscape,' he advised.

Opposite: The Ladies' Garden is enclosed by walls of local stone. *Clematis* and roses clamber over every surface: there is the climbing, cream-coloured rose 'Madame Alfred Carrière', along with the heavily scented 'Albéric Barbier', 'Félicité et Perpétue', 'Adélaide d'Orléans' and the violet-coloured 'Veilchenblau'.

The centrepiece of the gardens at Broughton is undoubtedly the Ladies' Garden, created in 1900 by Lady Lennox and, after World War II, updated with advice from the great American designer Lanning Roper (1912–1983). It is best viewed from the roof and parapets of the castle. High walls of gentle Cotswold stone, clothed in large-flowered hybrid clematis and old-fashioned roses, enclose this intimate 'garden room'. Open windows built into the walls allow tempting glimpses of the exuberant planting from outside.

Within the Ladies' Garden, a parterre in the shape of the fleur-de-lis is inscribed in well-clipped box, each segment filled with exuberant plantings of old-fashioned roses: the pale pink 'Gruss an Aachen' and the deeper pink 'Heritage'. The 'Rose De Rescht', a very double, scented old Damask rose with purple-red flowers and pink-grey foliage, creates a focal point in the centre of the arrangement. In the borders that hug the walls Hybrid Musk roses, including the highly scented Pemberton rose 'Felicia', along with the David Austin–bred 'Gertrude Jekyll' and the rugosa 'Roseraie de l'Haie', bloom with perennials, all spilling luxuriously onto the gravel paths, constrained only by perfectly clipped orbs in box. Standard hawthorns (*Crataegus* 'Paul's Scarlet' syn. 'Coccinea Plena') stand guard at the exits, adding height to the arrangement.

US novelist Henry James said of Broughton Castle, 'Perfection, what with moat, gatehouse, church and gorgeous orange and buff stone.' I couldn't agree more.

Great Fosters

*Really darling, you're lounging there sipping
vodka as though you were at Great Fosters.*

SIR NOËL COWARD (1899–1973), ENGLISH AUTHOR, ACTOR AND COMPOSER

What would you do if you were informed that a major road was planned to slice through your beloved garden, that soon thousands of cars would roar through your property each day? That was the horror that faced the owners of Great Fosters at Egham, Surrey, England, when told in the 1970s that the M25, the section of the orbital motorway connecting London to Heathrow airport and England's west counties, was to be built through a focal axis crucial to this important historic landscape.

Recent archaeology had revealed that Great Fosters—once known as Great Forresters—was part of the Royal Windsor Old Forest, playground of kings and queens, and incorporated an Elizabethan pile used by Henry VIII as a hunting lodge. The moated house once belonged to Jane Austen's brother. Then, for the first half of the twentieth century Great Fosters operated as a lavish hotel, the first 'country house hotel' in England, favoured by politicians, débutantes and film stars. (Charlie Chaplin kept a permanent suite of rooms there.)

Now, after lengthy negotiations with myriad local and national authorities, and more than a decade of restoration—following a master plan drawn up by landscape architect Kim Wilkie (b. 1955)—Great Fosters is again a five-star hotel, set in gardens that are surely among the best in the United Kingdom. Wilkie was called in to restore the historic grounds, regenerate important existing oak woodlands, rejuvenate stream corridors and create a vast new lake, thereby returning the intricate formal gardens to their magnificent Arts and Crafts incarnation. (The gardens—

Opposite: At Great Fosters, a 200-metre-long avenue of ancient limes connects the house with the turf amphitheatre, which features 6-metre-high bunds, protecting this important landscape and former royal playground from the visual and auditory implications of the M25.

inspired by those at Hampton Court and the revival of the fashion of topiary—had been laid out in the 1920s by the architect WH Romaine-Walker and Gilbert Jenkins, first president of the British Landscape Institute.)

Wilkie's solution to the noise and visual implications of the motorway was to construct a 6-metre high amphitheatre of terraced banks, sculpted from clay brought in from London and planted with rye grasses. A kilometre-long earth bund was also constructed along the motorway to support the arrangement. From the floor of the amphitheatre, reached from the house by a 200-metre-long grass avenue flanked with a double row of ancient limes, there is now no sight of and little sound from the multitude of cars steaming past just a few metres away.

Returning to the house through the parkland and wildflower meadows, tree-lined avenues give way to the Knot Garden, a quartet of formal parterres, laid out in the 1920s, and through which topiary peacocks strut. Each section houses a statue; at the centre is a sundial once owned by English admiral Sir Francis Drake. This extravagant garden, designed to reflect the intricate weavings of a Persian carpet—the traditional inspiration for knot and parterre patterns—is located within the confines of a Saxon moat, which dates from 500 AD and encloses the Elizabethan house.

Over several years, from 1991, the overgrown yews and box hedges in the Knot Garden, which constrain lavenders, catmint, sage and alliums, were successfully cut back to the hard wood.

Opposite, top: Great Fosters's glorious sunken rose garden. *Opposite, bottom:* A moat surrounds the formal gardens, reminding us that the property was once a royal park. *Above:* Dawn lights the façade of the seventeenth-century manor house, now a grand, country house hotel.

Top, left to right: Throughout Great Fosters intimate enclosed rooms, which employ plantings in different colour themes and which change with the seasons, afford tantalising glimpses of artworks. *Above:* A Japanese-style bridge crosses the Saxon moat to this summer house, and directs the visitor on to the glorious rose gardens. *Opposite:* The restored formal parterre and Knot Garden come into sharp focus when enjoyed from the roof. First laid out in the early twentieth century, more recent renovations, which employed severe pruning of the box hedges, have resulted in a triumphant design of restraint, combined with exuberance.

Best appreciated from the castellated tower of the house, the Knot Garden is connected to the sunken rose garden by a wisteria-swathed bridge—inspired by those of ancient Japanese gardens—across the moat.

The sunken Rose Garden—located in a large enclosure of yew hedges into which seats have been cut—is unimaginably beautiful at dawn, with the pale green misted light lingering above clouds of scented blossom. The varieties 'Perle d'Or', 'Albertine', 'Blossomtime', 'Wedding Day' and 'Kiftsgate' clambour over semi-circular pergolas on three sides. A central ellipse of hoops, covered in Pemberton-bred pink roses, protects a lily pond and classical fountain. As this area of the garden also dates from the 1920s, new roses were planted in cardboard boxes of fresh soil, to counter any disease problems that may have been residual in the ground. Eventually, of course, the cardboard rots and the roots of each plant reach into the soil.

The gardens at Great Fosters also contain intimate, hedged private rooms—one housing peonies, another iris, yet another devoted to blue flowers, and each set with an important piece of sculpture.

It has taken more than a decade, but these wonderful gardens have now been returned to their pre-war elegance and beauty and, with the house, are listed by English Heritage. Long-term management of the historic landscape includes the restoration and reafforestation of 25 hectares, acquired in the late twentieth century, which roll out from the lake.

The garden is close to Heathrow Airport but, as you sit on the sandstone terrace, wrapped in the gold of an English summer afternoon, breathing in these gardens, at once exciting, beautiful and historic, you won't want to go anywhere.

The
COLLECTORS' GARDENS

The dedication with which some hunt for antiquities, great works of art, rare books, or trophies that celebrate sporting prowess, is common to all collectors. Gardeners are no exception. Plant hunters of the eighteenth and nineteenth centuries put their lives at great risk seeking the botanical treasures of the New World for an insatiable gardening public in Europe and the United Kingdom. Today, plantspeople look for such bounty throughout a smaller universe, but with no less commitment.

Some gardeners spend a lifetime in research and study to gather a collection of one genus: their dedication is noted by the organisations for national collections, which go by various titles in different countries. Other gardeners cannot discipline themselves to a handful of genera and would grow one of every species, given the space. Some collectors are restrained; others plant with complete exuberance. All are united by the passion for collecting.

Isola Bella
AND
Isola Madre

The beautiful day was just declining when we came upon Lago Maggiore, with its lovely island. For however fanciful and fantastic Isola Bella may be, and is, it is still beautiful. Anything that springs out of that blue water, with the scenery around it, must be.

ENGLISH NOVELIST CHARLES DICKENS (1812–1870)

Dickens, Edith Wharton, George Sitwell and Henry James were among the throng of American and British literati that descended upon northern Italy's Lakes in the late nineteenth and early twentieth centuries to savour their 'air of perennial loveliness', as Wharton enthused.

Surrounded by mountains capped with snow for much of the year, Lake Maggiore is considered by many to be the most picturesque of these lakes. It is a little less frenetic than its neighbour, Lake Como, but no less dramatic. Extending into Switzerland, Lake Maggiore has long been a holiday destination for the privileged and for expatriates who created grand gardens around its shores.

Two islands, Isola Bella and Isola Madre, float jewel-like in Lake Maggiore's cerulean water and enjoy a climate several degrees milder than on the shore. They have been owned by the Borromeo family of bankers since the early sixteenth century.

Opposite: Designed from the first half of the seventeenth century by the Milanese architect Angelo Crivelli as a galleon in search of the treasures of the new world, Isola Bella rises dramatically from the blue waters of Lake Maggiore.

Italian gardens are complete works of art, encompassing all the disciplines: the study of history, architecture, sculpture, theatre and performance, imagination, and horticulture. Isola Bella—the site of Count Carlo Borromeo's seventeenth century villa—is a beguiling confection built across the entire island in ten terraces, which support a dazzling collection of statues placed at dramatic vantage points throughout the garden to overlook the lake. Terraces are retained by balustrades that also provide a setting for ornamentation and mark a boundary between land and space; the finite and the infinite.

The spectacular gardens on Isola Bella have always been used by the family as a show-piece for entertaining, while nearby Isola Madre, the site of a family home, is the repository of horticultural treasures from around the globe. In Italy, just as in the United Kingdom, plant hunters were sponsored by leading families who received, in return, dividends in the form of seeds of the botanical bounty.

The garden on Isola Madre is probably most famous for its collection of more than 800 different camellias, some of which are more than 150 years old. The banks of the salmon-pink, large-flowered *Camellia japonica* 'Drama Girl', the peony-form *C. j.* 'Tomorrow' and the pink-and-red-striped 'Tomorrow's Dawn' are breathtaking. Others are severely clipped to form narrow hedges, which soften extensive stone walls; some are pruned to create walkways.

A Kashmir cypress (*Cupressus cashmeriana*) of heroic dimensions—at more than 30 metres the tallest in Europe—is more than 200 years old. Its long, glaucous branches weep softly to the ground in front of the palazzo, which was renovated into its present incarnation in the early sixteenth century by the architect Pellegrino Pellegrini (1527–1592).

A clutch of now mature *Magnolia grandiflora* has been clipped and espaliered into a summer-house. The rare bigleaf magnolia (*Magnolia macrophylla*) flowers in May. There is a variety of bamboo, including towering stands of golden bamboo and the more delicate

Opposite: The *palazzo* on Isola Bella has hosted some historic meetings. In April 1935, with the threat from Hitler increasing, the music room saw an alliance signed between Italy's Mussolini, France's Pierre Laval and Great Britain's Ramsay McDonald, in an effort to prevent the outbreak of World War II. And Napoleon slept here on 17 August 1797, and visited again in 1801. *Above, left:* White peacocks strut the lawns of Isola Bella. *Above, centre:* The weather god, Jupiter, stands tall at Isola Bella, holding the bolt of lightning that has destroyed his enemies. Well-weathered terracotta pots house clipped domes of *Buxus*. Urns are decorated with three rings to signify the three names connected by marriage through all aspects of Italian life: Sforza, Visconti and Borromeo. *Above, right:* Terraces of roses lead to views that extend over the southern part of the lake from Isola Bella. A collection of Hybrid Tea roses—corals with oranges and reds with pinks—are underplanted with perennials. The pink-and-yellow-flowering *Rosa* 'Mutabilis' hugs the walls.

Above: The exotic atmosphere at Isola Madre is enhanced by plantings in the Palm Avenue, including the Chinese fan palm (*Trachycarpus fortunei*) and the Mediterranean fan palm, *Chamaerops humilis*. **Opposite:** The Isola Madre palazzo was renovated into its present incarnation in the early sixteenth century by the architect Pellegrino Pellegrini.

black. Plantings of callistemon, casuarina and eucalyptus from Australia abound, the latter filling the air with its unmistakable scent.

A walk around the perimeter of the island reveals swaths of hostas growing wild over the steep cliffs of seeping rock, upon which the house and garden are built. Spanish moss (*Tillandsia usneoides*), an epiphyte seen in old gardens in the deep south of the United States, drips in festoons from the cinnamon-covered branches of a twisted, 100-year-old *Myrtus communis*. In April and May banks of azaleas and rhododendrons bloom, and walkways are covered in flowering wisteria.

Adored by the English and the Americans, whether on a Grand Tour of Learning or as a place of rest, Lake Maggiore and its fantasy gardens are most eloquently described by writers and artists who, like Henry James, were captivated by 'that element of the rich and strange for the love of which one revisits Italy'.

Newby Hall

Aristocrats of ancient lineage, possessed of many superlative qualities ... They have the largest flowers ... no other genus can boast so many excellences. Their free-flowering character and great beauty of blossom and foliage are equalled by the ease with which they many be cultivated.

PLANT HUNTER ERNEST 'CHINESE' WILSON (1876–1930), WRITING OF THE MAGNOLIAS HE DISCOVERED IN CHINA

The approach to Newby Hall, near Ripon, Yorkshire, in the north of England, should be made very slowly to appreciate one of the loveliest parks you are likely to encounter. Sheep rest under ancient, spreading horse chestnut trees, while the elegant, pink brick Queen Anne house—home to the Compton family since 1748—beckons in the distance.

A double avenue of the white horse chestnuts leads you to the house: they replace earlier linden trees that feature in an eighteenth-century drawing by Dutch printmaker Johannes Kip (1653–1752) who, with his colleague Leonard Knyff, painted and engraved views of the great country houses throughout England. Their exquisitely detailed works provide the most accurate record of the splendour of post-Tudor and Stuart gardens, before the plantings were swept away in the landscaping fervour of Lancelot 'Capability' Brown and his disciples in the second half of the eighteenth century (*see* pages 15–19). The Kip drawing of the Newby estate depicts formal gardens, with a tree-lined axis from which several paths radiate, and orchards and vegetable gardens reaching down to the

Opposite: The elegant Newby Hall, built between 1690 and 1695, rests on its stone terrace, with its 'Wood Nymph' statue and lily pond, all encased in mellow stone balustrading; this elevation faces south, towards the famous twin herbaceous borders and the River Ure.

Above: In May, Newby Hall's sublime twin herbaceous borders are beginning to show the promise of their main summer drama. Backed with clipped hedges of yew (*Taxus baccata*), they form the gardens' focal point. While successfully employing architectural plants such as the cardoons to lend structure in spring, the complicated arrangements of asters, delphiniums, clove-scented dianthus, and more than forty species of *Salvia*, are all at their peak by midsummer. **Opposite:** The rock garden—particularly fashionable in the Victorian era—today houses bog garden treasures, from swaths of the covetable *Primula japonica*, to astilbes and precious ferns, including the elegant Lady Fern. Here, the burgundy-leaved *Acer palmatum* grows beneath the white-flowered *Olearia* × *scilloniensis*, and the North American gooseberry, *Ribes speciosum*, is planted so that its red, hanging flowers can be appreciated. A stone aqueduct carries water to the cascade beyond.

River Ure. Influenced by French formality, the earliest gardens at Newby were designed with the help of George London (1681–1714)—of the famous firm London & Wise—who had worked with André Le Nôtre (1613–1700), perhaps the most important landscaper of the seventeenth century, responsible for the vistas of the Champs Élysées and the redesign of the famous French palaces Versailles and Fontainebleau.

The gardens seen today are largely the creation of the current owner's grandfather, Major Edward Compton, renovated and embellished by his son, Robin Compton, and his wife, Janey, from 1977.

There are many ways to explore this 15-hectare garden. One is through the Statue Walk, designed by the architect William Burges (1827–1881) in the late nineteenth century. From here the main axis of the garden draws you on—a wide grass path that leads from an expansive terrace on which the house rests, between mirrored perennial borders, south to the river. Smaller, enclosed gardens—each with a different 'feel' and housing different plantings—are laid out on either side of this central axis. Each is entered through a 'gateway' cut into the high yew hedges that back the borders.

There is also the Autumn Garden, on the site of a former croquet lawn and planted with dahlias, verbenas, salvias and other late-flowering perennials; the Holly Garden, with its holm oak (*Quecus ilex*); the Beacon Garden, housing a tribute to the Queen's Jubilee year;

and the Rock Garden. There are two rose gardens, one of which is devoted to the Wars of the Roses, where *R. gallica* var. *officinalis* (also known as the red rose of Lancaster) flowers with the white *R. rugosa* 'Alba'; the luscious pink-and-white striped *R. mundi*; or *R. gallica* 'Versicolor' which, you might imagine, has been splashed with raspberries and cream.

Newby Hall holds the national collection of dogwoods (*Cornus* spp.), one of 640 national collections of genera in the United Kingdom, held for the National Council for the Conservation of Plants and Gardens (NCCPG), of which Robin Compton is president. There are more than 100 dogwoods in the Newby gardens, including *Cornus* 'Eddie's White Wonder', with its elegant layered branches that hold bracts like large, white, resting butterflies. It was bred by Henry M Eddie in his river-side nursery in Vancouver, Canada, in the 1930s. When his nursery flooded it was the only plant he was able to save: all the trees today come from that one specimen. The Newby collection includes the glorious pagoda dogwood (*C. alternifolia* 'Argentea') with its variegated foliage on tiered branches, and the beautifully shaped *C. controversa* from Japan, Taiwan and China. *C. kousa* 'Norman Hadden', 'Milky Way', 'Madame Butterfly' and 'Satomi' are also part of the collection.

Robin Compton's favourite part of the garden is the Wild Garden, where a collection of maples are particularly cherished for their bark, including the paper bark maple (*Acer griseum*), with its peeling, cinnamon-coloured bark. It was discovered in 1901 in China by the plant hunter Ernest 'Chinese' Wilson (1876–1930) who, admits Robin Compton, is 'my pin-up boy'. This section of the garden has been dubbed 'Wilson's Corner' and houses many of the treasures Wilson introduced to the west. There is *Rhododendron orbiculare,* with its trusses of pink, bell-like flowers, and *R. auriculatum*, sporting huge leaves and white flowers late in the season.

The Wild Garden is also home to *R. fortuneii*, which holds elegant buds that open pale pink; *R. falconeri*, offering scented cream flowers and flaking brown bark; and *R. schlippenbachii*, with leaves that take on bronze tones in autumn. There is also the lovely *R. campylocarpum* hybrid 'Dairymaid', which blooms in a froth of cream to pink.

A copse of white-barked birch (*Betula utilis* var. *jacquemontii*)—underplanted with a swath of the beautiful Solomon's Seal, their nodding white bells held on arching stems—gleams nearby. Good use is made of ground covers—*Geranium macrorrhizum* and *Persicaria affinis* help reduce weeding.

The scale of the different garden enclosures and spaces, and the use of perspective—for which Robin Compton pays tribute to his father, whom he applauds also for his synergy and sense of balance—are among the many admirable aspects of the Newby Hall gardens. Grand expanses are in keeping with the important house and the size of the entire gardens, but virtuoso planting schemes within each area—all overseen by a passionate plantsman—have ensured that these gardens remain intensely personal and intimate.

Top: Sylvia's Garden, set into a sunken stone terrace, was created for Robin Compton's mother in the 1920s as a series of eight rectangles, planted to peak in May for the York races. The beds are filled with statuesque alliums, delphiniums and iris, complemented by peonies, including 'Sarah Bernhardt', 'Duchesse de l'Amour' and 'Bowl of Beauty'. Corners are marked with clipped orbs of the coral berry (*Symphoricarpos orbiculatus*), valued for its small white berries flushed with pink. Tightly clipped pyramids of box add structure to the garden in winter. Ground covers of species geraniums include the easy-going 'Brookside', with its constant mass of small lilac flowers; there is also the very blue *Lithodora diffusa* along with *Veronica gentianoides*, a matt-forming perennial that flowers with spires of a paler blue. ***Bottom, left to right***: The gardens' last remaining avenue of European limes (*Tilia x europaea*), planted in 1696; this fountain urn is the central focus of the Autumn Garden; *Clematis montana* 'Rubens' on a rose pergola; a 300-year-old copper beech.

Rowallane

As kingfishers catch fire, dragonflies draw flame;
As tumbled over rim in roundy wells
Stones ring; like each tucked string tells, each hung bell's
Bow swung finds tongue to fling out broad its name;
Each mortal thing does one thing and the same …

GERARD MANLEY HOPKINS, 'AS KINGFISHERS CATCH FIRE,
DRAGONFLIES DRAW FLAME', VERSE 1, LINES 1–5

Have you ever seen a ribbon of the Himalayan blue poppy, flowering its brilliant blue by the hundreds, its colour intensifying as the early morning lights upon dew-covered, shimmering, crêpe-paper petals and downy, lime green leaves? My first sighting of this most coveted of plants, *Meconopsis betonicifolia,* was one July some years ago at Rowallane, a garden of rare and tender treasures in Northern Ireland.

A plantsman's garden of some 20 hectares not far from Belfast, Rowallane is better known, in fact, for the collection of rhododendrons that was started by Hugh Armytage Moore in 1903, when he inherited the property from his uncle, the Reverend John Moore. Named Rowallane after the family seat in Scotland, the house—completed in 1861—is now the headquarters of the Northern Ireland chapter of the National Trust, which is entrusted with maintaining the gardens.

The grounds are entered by a long drive that winds beneath towering conifers—of specimens such as the North American *Chamaecyparis nootkatensis*; the Chinese *Tsuga yunnanensis* and *Cupressus lusitanica*

Opposite: At Rowallane, the voluptuous plantings of the Walled Garden include the National Collection of large-flowered penstemons. The Walled Garden is reached through a shadowy avenue of beech and rhododendron, which gives way to carefully clipped sentinels of Irish yew.

'Glauca Pendula'—past granite cairns and stone seats. It is tempting to rush on towards the famous collections of perennials; take time, however, to appreciate the peaceful, cathedral-like atmosphere of the entrance.

A dozen closely clipped Irish yew (*Taxus baccata* 'Fastigiata') lead into the walled garden. This former kitchen garden is now an Aladdin's cave of horticultural treasures nurtured in the benign microclimate and acid soil. Candelabra primulas in great, colourful swaths—including *P.* 'Rowallane Rose' and the carmine 'Miller's Crimson'—are backlit with the delicate, light green foliage of the deciduous royal fern *Osmunda regalis*. And the national collection of large-flowered penstemons—including the purple 'Sour Grapes', 'Garnet' and 'Burgundy'—flowers through spring and summer.

Great drifts of *Kirengeshoma palmata*, with its spires of creamy flowers, provide a backbone to masses of rogersias, flowering in creams, and pale and dark pinks. Also in the mix is a Bressingham form of *Rheum palmatum* 'Atrosanguineum', a decorative rhubarb with a brilliant green leaf that is a rich burgundy on the underside, bred by the famed Norfolk-based nursery. The exuberant plantings are punctuated with clipped obelisks and tripods of yew.

Opposite, top: Rowallane's walled garden was once the kitchen garden but now boasts a treasure chest of species that thrive in the garden's benign microclimate and acid soil. *Opposite, bottom:* Topiarised Irish yew punctuate the spaces in the walled garden. *Above:* A stately avenue of clipped Irish yew (*Taxus baccata* 'Fastigiata') leads into the walled garden.

Above, left to right: *Meconopsis betonicifolia*; *Mahonia* × *media*; the very scented, deep carmine Moss rose 'Tuscany Superb'; the tree peony, *Paeonia suffruticosa* 'Souvenir de Maxime Cornu'. *Opposite:* Hostas, peonies, purple-leaved *Berberis* and heritage roses thrive—as do primulas, viburnums and rhododendrons—within the protection of the garden walls.

A feature of the walled garden is the spectacular *Viburnum plicatum* f. *tomentosum* 'Rowallane', its elegant layers of horizontal branches covered in June with white blossom, like an exaggerated, multi-tiered wedding cake.

In the outer walled garden, collections of species hydrangeas, fuchsias and climbing and shrub roses keep the performance fascinating throughout summer. There are also collections of heather and tiny alpine and Mediterranean bulbs.

Many of the plants at Rowallane—including the multi-trunked *Rhododendron* 'Shilsonii', coveted for its cinnamon-coloured, smooth bark; the fascinating *R. macabeanum* with its huge, felt-backed leaves and trusses of yellow flowers blotched with purple; and *R. basilicum* wearing cinnamon-backed leaves—were raised from seed collected by the most famous of the nineteenth- and twentieth-century plant hunters—Ernest 'Chinese' Wilson, George Forrest and Frank Kingdon-Ward—and through Armytage Moore's contacts at the Edinburgh Botanic Gardens.

Outside the walled garden, a gently undulating woodland shelters more rhododendrons—planted in groups and copses as nature might have placed them in the wild—and trees and shrubs from the subcontinent, the Americas, Australia and New Zealand. Beyond are wildflower meadows. Collections of magnolia, like the yellow-flowering *M. acuminata*, dogwoods, a magnificent handkerchief or dove tree (*Davidia involucrata*), a massive specimen of the wonderfully scented mountain ribbonwood (*Hoheria lyallii*) from New Zealand, and stands of rowan and beech ensure that the treats and surprises constantly unfold.

Singapore

BOTANIC

Gardens

In the marsh pink orchid's faces
With their coy and dainty graces,
Lure us to their hiding places—
Laugh, O murmuring Spring!

SARAH FOSTER DAVIS, 'SUMMER SONG'

Singapore is a great place for garden-lovers. The entire island is a lush, tropical garden: historic jungles with treetop walks skirt the city and avenues of tall trees shade streets resplendent with colourful plantings that form central buffers separating lanes of traffic. Even Changi Airport is filled with spectacular displays of orchids, and swaths of covetable torch gingers erupt from lush tapestries of boldly painted foliage in hotel gardens. The city is clean, green, safe and a fascinating mix of more than a handful of races.

During the 1960s the government started planting the tall-growing, umbrella-shaped rain trees (*Samanea saman*) that now form tunnels of cool green over the roads; verges and carriageways are softened with scaled-up blocks of gingers, ribbons of ixoras and the Madagascan flaming

Opposite: The indigenous sealing wax palm (*Cyrtostachys renda*), also dubbed the lipstick palm, frames one of several lakes in the Singapore Botanic Gardens. With their sheaths of brilliant vermillion—considered a lucky colour in the East—this palm is a symbol of Singapore.

Above: The *Dendrobium* White Fairy is shaded by *Phyllanthus pectinatus* trees, sporting beautiful mottled, cinnamon-coloured bark.
Opposite, top: This delicate bandstand is the oldest structure in the gardens. The British military band played here, on the full moon of each month, from 1860 until the 1930s.
Opposite centre, left to right: The cannonball tree (*Couroupita guianensis*); the beautiful hanging parrot, *Heliconia rostrata* 'Sexy Pink' from the Zingiberales group; the flowers of the torch ginger (*Etlingera elatior*) are used in cooking. **Bottom:** The Evolution Garden, housing ancient prehistoric cycads, spells out more than 3000 million years of botanical history (the first 1000 million years had no plant life). Designed to demonstrate that fossil fuels are derived from plants, this garden displays related plants from the period of coal swamps during the Carboniferous period. Cycads represent the final years of the Fern period, the time of the dinosaurs and *Araucaria* genus. The first primitive flowering plants—including magnolias and water lilies—developed after the Gymnosperms.

beauty (*Carphalea kirondron*) in harlequin colours. Frangipani blooms, in red, pink, yellow and white, on contorted branches overhead; apricot, pink or white bracts of *Mussaenda* hybrids flutter in the breeze. Flowering bougainvilleas cascade from overpasses, and orchids and ferns flourish in the forks and on trunks of trees.

At the heart of the city are the Botanic Gardens, established in 1859 on the site of an abandoned plantation. They are much loved for their heritage trees, some pre-dating the gardens' establishment. An icon here is the native tembusu (*Fagraea fragrans*), a tree with low, sweeping branches. According to Director Dr Chin See Chung, many Singaporeans remember sitting on this tree as children; now they bring their grandchildren. The hard wood of the tembusu is used for chopping boards throughout the Malay Peninsula, and the tree features on the five-dollar note.

Among the many botanical stars in the gardens is the cannonball tree (*Couroupita guianensis*); its sweetly scented apricot-to-pink blooms, reminiscent of giant quince blossom, appear on long stems that wrap the trunk. One of the most arresting is the Pride of Burma (*Amherstia nobilis*), coveted for its cascades of red and gold orchid-like flowers, which hang like chandeliers. (And, as was the habit of many great British families in the eigtheenth and nineteenth centuries, the 6th Duke of Devonshire sent his twenty-year-old gardening apprentice, John Gibson, to India in 1835 to obtain this treasure—then unknown in Europe— for the great conservatory on his magnificent Derbyshire estate, Chatsworth).

A relative of the brazil nut, the monkey-pot tree (*Lecythis ollaria*) develops huge, urn-shaped fruit. In the gardens it plays host to a selection of ferns, including the bird's nest fern

BOTANICAL NOMENCLATURE

The naming of orchid hybrids is an exception to the rule of botanical nomenclature: orchid hybrid names, known as grex epithets, are registered with the Royal Horticultural Society (RHS) in London. All hybrids, whether humanmade or naturally occurring, *do not attract single quotes*. For instance, the hybrid between the two *Coelogyne* species, *cristata* and *flaccida* is always called *Coelogyne* Unchained Melody. No single inverted commas are used, as it is not a cultivar; it is a hybrid. Selected clones of this hybrid may be granted cultivar names—these differentiate related, but slightly different, plants. So you could have, for instance, *Coelogyne* Unchained Melody 'Mary'.

To further check on parentage of orchids, go to www.rhs.org. uk/plants/registerpages/orchid_parentage.asp

(*Asplenium nidus*) and the smaller-leafed tongue fern, *Pyrrosia longifolia*. As Singapore has one of the highest incidents of lightning strikes per unit of land in the world, more than 120 trees in the gardens are protected with copper cables, which run up the trees and record strikes.

A series of boardwalks is being constructed through the Valley of the Giants—6 hectares of original rainforest. Cast in geo-textile concrete to imitate old railway sleepers, these strong, sustainable walkways allow visitors to enjoy the ancient species without compacting the soil by their tramping.

Palm Valley, an outdoor performance area, overlooks a soaring, flower-shaped concert stage. There, the fishtail palm (*Caryota mitis*) flowers from its crown with a long inflorescence from which a mass of seeds, like thousands of small beads strung on tassels, hang. The stemless Joey palm (*Johannesteijsmannia altifrons*) rises like a huge shuttlecock; the black fibres that wrap the sugar palm (*Arenga pinnata*) are harvested in the Malay Peninsula for ropes, brushes and thatching and were once used to line dykes in Holland. The lawn that carpets this space is of the tropical, broad-leaved cow grass (*Axonopus compressus*); it copes with humidity and high rainfall but, as it is fast growing, demands regular mowing.

The Singapore Botanic Gardens house a collection of tropical clumping bamboos, including a massive stand of the giant *Bambusa bambos*, replete with steel-hard thorns, and the more gentle *Bambusa multiplex*, often used for hedging.

The vast collection of colourful genera from the Zingiberales group—from the beautiful hanging parrot *Heliconia rostrata* 'Sexy Pink' to the perky psittacorums—are edged in a variety of lush calatheas. With their stardust markings in silvers, greys, yellows and greens, they make the ultimate tapestry plant.

But one of the most exciting areas in these lovely gardens is the famous collection of orchids. Arranged throughout several hectares are more than 400 orchid species and hundreds of hybrids blooming in a wide palette of pastels, as well as vibrant reds and oranges. Planned to reflect four seasons, the Orchid Garden houses Singapore's national flower, the climbing *Vanda* Miss Joaquim, as well as terrestrial orchids, such as the little yellow *Spathaglotis* hybrids. The collection of epiphytic orchids, including species of *Mokara*, *Ascocenda*, *Aranthera*, *Renantanda*, *Dendrobium*, *Brassavola*, *Oncidium* and *Epidendrum*, demand a well-drained environment, so are planted in charcoal or broken bricks among bark upon the ground or are attached to trees. And the cool house protects fragile species, including the slipper plants (*Paphiopedilum* spp.) from Malaysia.

It is with good reason that orchid-lovers return time and time again to enjoy this virtuoso collection.

Opposite: In front of the world-famous Orchid Garden, the lawn is bordered by multi-hued orchids and lush tropical foliage. The Nibung palm (Oncosperma tigillarium) towers above an underplanting of the orange-flowered Mokara Chitti Gold, and a swath of alpinias. Frangipanis throughout the Singapore Botanic Gardens include the evergreen Plumeria obtusa, native to the Bahamas.

Nooroo

Tomorrow again they will be there.
The multiple silence of their noise
Vibrates with glittering leaves, atoms of trees
Ranked up the enclosing hiss, the restless glare
Of sea, the dazzling beach, and those who lie
Tranced like them, in thronging vacancy.

JR ROWLAND, 'CICADAS', VERSE 4

About a two-hour drive west of Sydney lies Mount Wilson, one of Australia's most exciting garden regions. Mount Wilson is a tiny village of exquisite gardens perched atop a small volcanic outcrop of rich red soil on the northern end of the Blue Mountains, part of the Great Dividing Range—a rib that runs from the furthest point of tropical Queensland to Melbourne in the south, and beneath the Bass Strait to Tasmania. An area of just a couple of dozen properties, the village is centred on only a few streets and boasts some of Australia's best gardens.

While not many of us can own a garden on the grand scale of these, it is, nevertheless, uplifting to see the treasures that have been collected by generations of devoted owners over more than a century. There is plenty that can be learned from these gardens, even if your botanical bounty is confined to a small city plot or to a collection of containers on a balcony.

One such garden is Nooroo, looking wonderful under the directorship of owners Drs Anthony and Lorraine Barrett, who purchased the property from the much-revered botanist Dr Peter Valder in 1992. Nooroo was

Opposite: In mid October when visiting Nooroo, it is tempting to rush past the special *Clematis*, rhododendrons and tree ferns close to the front garden, to see the pergola, which is resplendent with *Wisteria floribunda* 'Macrobotrys', boasting racemes that reach up to a metre.

originally taken up by the pastoralist William Hay in 1880 and was developed further by the Valder family over seventy-five years. While the new owners are sensitive to the provenance of the garden, some change has been inevitable. Fences have been removed, and areas that were sheep paddocks have been opened up to new plantings of deciduous azaleas, dogwoods and maples to augment mature chestnuts, beech and oak. Careful tree surgery and some judicious removal of trees that had reached their senescence have only added to the success of the garden.

The plantings just inside the entrance to Nooroo, which is located down a quiet, shaded, winding lane, are a good aperitif for the rest of the garden. At the front gate, rough tree ferns (*Cyathea australis*), thought to be more than 200 years old and emblematic of Mount Wilson, are wreathed in white wisteria and *Clematis montana*, *C.* 'Ernest Markham' and 'King Leopold of the Belgians'.

These front beds, which are encased in local rock, house miniature lacecap hydrangeas and several varieties of lily-of-the-valley and, growing around a small, rectangular pool, Louisiana iris and the prized candelabra primula, *Primula sikkimensis*.

In late October, however, only the most self-controlled would not hurry to see the spectacular wisteria (*Wisteria floribunda* 'Macrobotrys'), its opulent display of long racemes framing the front door of the pit-sawn timber house that dates from 1880.

The vistas in the garden are particularly successful, not only because of the different textures and shapes created by the plantings of oak, ash, elm, chestnut and rhododendron,

Opposite, top: In the dramatic 'wisteria court' in October—a gravel area covering a disused tennis court—there are twenty-eight standard wisteria, of twelve different varieties. After careful pruning, all are flowering wonderfully and it is now possible to walk beneath the branches of these mature specimens with their thick, twisting trunks. The Japanese iris on the court are colour-coded to match the wisteria. Here, the white wisteria is *W. brachybotrys* 'Shiro-kapitan'; flowering a pink to lilac is *Wisteria floribunda* 'Kuchi-beni'. *Opposite centre, left to right:* On the wisteria court, tubs of a hybrid *Rhododendron yakushimanum* flowers white beneath the wisteria; *Wisteria* 'Purple Splendour'; *W. floribunda* 'Kuchi-beni'. *Opposite, bottom:* *Wisteria floribunda* 'Kuchi-beni'. *Above:* Deep edgings of lily-of-the-valley (*Convallaria majalis*), which love the warmth provided by the stone wall.

Above: The famed pergola at Nooroo that supports *Wisteria floribunda* 'Macrobotrys'. Rhododedrons, azaleas, maples and *Clematis* thrive in the microclimate created by soaring eucalypts, tree ferns and a collection of exotic trees. *Opposite, top*: The charming wooden cottage at Nooroo viewed across a sea of spring bluebells. *Opposite, bottom*: A quiet spot among azaleas and rhododendrons. On the right, the flowering *Rhododendron yakushimanum* reaches its peak in October.

which cluster around the edges of the garden pictures, but also because of the expanses of beautifully maintained lawn, which balance the scene.

Even after many seasons at Nooroo, the Barretts continue to discover treasures. Recently a mature *Abies forrestii,* native to western China, was discovered among the collection of conifers: it bears cobalt-blue cones and is rare in Australia. A variety of hollies with exotically coloured berries was also found.

The garden, with its distinctive white-painted summer-house, spectacular wisteria and leafy glades, has featured on an Australian two-dollar stamp. This, and the fact that so much has been written about this wonderful garden, means that visiting Nooroo is rather like communing with a beloved friend.

ARTISTS' GARDENS

Garden-making, perhaps the most indulgent of pleasures, is surely the most difficult of art forms. A garden never stands still, and plants rarely behave as expected. The reality—as the garden grows and pleases itself—often appears very different from the garden of the imagination. But artists—from designers to decorators, painters, sculptors or composers—with their innate grasp of tone and texture, colour and combination, movement and form—seem to combine all these considerations to create successfully and effortlessly. The result is gardens that are original, often unique, and written in the vernacular of their place; they are places of great beauty.

Woodbridge

No element of landscape design is more potent than a stretch of water giving serenity to a scene. It has the same simplifying effect on the landscape that is given by a covering of snow; the trivialities are smoothed away. All objects are enhanced by their reflection ... by their repetition in the water.

DAME SYLVIA CROWE, *TOMORROW'S LANDSCAPE*, P. 152

Woodbridge is a magnificent 5-hectare garden—just north of Auckland, in New Zealand's north island—which incorporates rolling lawns, lakes edged with bog-garden plants, rose gardens, a virtuoso vegetable garden and a collection of succulents and dry-garden species. This is a garden for the landscape designer as well as those fascinated with rare and unusual plants. It is also a decorator's garden; Christine Peek, who has developed Woodbridge with her husband, Tony, since 1991, has a happy knack of combining colours, tones, textures and shapes in a most effective way.

An arch resplendent in spring and summer with the large-flowering, deep purple *Clematis* 'Niobe', flowering with the chestnut-coloured, double *Rosa roxburghii,* leads into the garden by way of the Potager. There, trellises of broad beans and kiwi fruit are offset by collectors' plants like the climbing red nasturtium 'Empress of India'. Then, a small door set in a high wall opens into the main garden to reveal sweeping lawns—in a mixture of fescue and creeping bent—bound on one side by a high hedge of the silver-toned *Cupressus arizonica* 'Blue Ice.'

Opposite: The entrance to the garden at Woodbridge is cut into a dense cypress hedge and framed in cascades of the purple-to-cerise multiflora rambling rose 'Violette'. Roses, clematis and wisteria romp over pergolas and screens in this garden to create a constant performance in colour and scent.

Beyond, a croquet lawn is separated from the main part of the garden by a long pergola covered in the climbing white rose 'Albéric Barbier'. Sometimes called the gardenia rose, even though it has the scent of apples, this double, white-flowered beauty—almost ever-green—is seen growing wild on the roadsides throughout New Zealand. Christine has had a soft spot for it since she was a young girl.

In front of the long, low homestead, a wide, semi-circular terrace provides a home for a collection of water-wise sedums and echeverias in tones of bronze, red, cerise and pink. The perennial russet-flowering *Achillea* 'Salmon Beauty' blooms are accompanied by *Sedum* 'Autumn Joy', with its dusky pink summer heads that darken to bronze through autumn; there is also *Euphorbia* 'Blue Peace' and a mass of the grey-leaved succulent *Echeveria* × *imbricata*, which produces red trumpet-like blooms in spring.

Opposite, top: The beautiful and the useful come together in The Potager at Woodbridge. *Opposite, bottom left to right*: Honeysuckle and roses frame doorways between garden 'rooms'; a long pergola covered in the climbing white rose 'Albéric Barbier'; the large-flowered, cerise *Clematis* 'Niobe' flowers with the burgundy-to-chestnut-coloured double *Rosa roxburghii*. *Above*: Hedges of lavender and westringia are teamed with roses on a gently sloping site, which affords views over the garden.

Opposite: Around the water gardens at
Woodbridge, angelica, the giant ornamental
rhubarb (*Gunnera manicata*), hostas, grasses
and taro thrive in the dappled shade offered
by the swamp cypress (*Taxodium distichum*)
and self-sown native tree ferns.

Two *Wisteria floribunda* 'Macrobotrys', displaying their metre-long racemes of scented lilac flowers each October, cover metal trellises constructed on either end of the terrace that feeds off the sitting-room; for Christine, their beauty is enough to invoke tears.

A flight of generously proportioned steps centred on the terrace points towards the lake. Fed by springs from the higher reaches of the valley, these water gardens eventually become the Mahoenui Stream, emptying into Waitemata Harbour. This damp area is edged with a wide ribbon of *Iris sibirica* 'Caesar's Brother', which flowers a deep blue each November. The luscious angelica, sporting glossy, ruffled leaves, and the giant ornamental rhubarb (*Gunnera manicata*) are teamed with the soft grey of that so-smart grass *Miscanthus sinensis* 'Morning Light'. They all thrive in the dappled shade cast by self-sown native tree ferns, mostly tall-growing mamaku or black ponga (*Cyathea medullaris*) and silver tree ferns (*Cyathea dealbata*) with their silver-frosted filigreed branches, and of the swamp cypress (*Taxodium distichum*). A wide ribbon of the black-stemmed taro (*Calocasia esculenta* 'Black Magic') thrives by the bog garden: while it can become rampant, it is kept in check by autumn frosts. It looks striking growing with ribbons of hosta: 'Albomarginata' or 'Albopicta', along with 'Loyalist'.

Roses are revered in this garden, as are clematis, and the two are planted together to cover screens, arbours and pergolas. The clematis hide the 'bare legs' of the climbing roses, create exciting colour combinations, and extend the flowering season. The old rose 'Fantin Latour' blooms with a large-flowered lilac clematis, a Hadley hybrid, and with *R.* 'Bloomfield Abundance'. There is *C.* 'Belle of Woking', a blowsy, double, silver-mauve that always attracts compliments, and *C. napaulensis*, winter flowering with clusters of cream flowers and gorgeous purple stamens. *C. orientalis*, a soft honey yellow loved for its silky seedpods, grows through a banksian rose. C. 'Rouge Cardinal' twines through the multiflora rambling rose 'Violette', a similar but darker rose than 'Veilchenblau', which is splashed with creams and pinks, as well as purple.

A cream-painted summer-house supports the clotted-cream colours of *Rosa* 'Buff Beauty', blooming with 'Claire Jacquier'; the yellow climbing rose 'Alchymist' blooms with 'Félicité et Perpétue'. There is a sense of great expectation in this garden—and for Tony and Christine, always something to look forward to.

Suffolk sheep graze peacefully beyond the post-and-rail fence, which separates the garden from the verdant paddocks surrounding it, for New Zealand is blessed with plentiful rain.

Christine is an admirer of the work of English garden designer and author Beth Chatto (b. 1923), who is renowned for her belief in planting in generous blocks to create an effective underlying structure or grid to which she adds the stars of the horticultural world. Christine has aimed for big groups of plants of different textures and foliages—even without the flowers—to create a tapestry or patchwork effect. She has succeeded admirably.

La Mortella

The great art in landscaping is the invisible order: the harmony impressed on the layout by the architect.

RUSSELL PAGE, *THE EDUCATION OF A GARDENER*, P. 26

In 1948 the 46-year-old English composer William Walton was in Buenos Aires, Argentina, to attend a conference. While there he met the 22-year-old Susana Gil; within a fortnight they were engaged. The married couple moved from London to Ischia, a rocky island that erupts from the blue waters of the Mediterranean in the Bay of Naples. There, in this tranquil setting, William wrote music; Susana set about creating a garden. With the help of Russell Page (*see* page 223), perhaps the most influential designer of the twentieth century, she built La Mortella, a haven of botanical bounty from around the world.

Today, you arrive by ferry from Sorrento or Naples and then taxi through the town of Forio to a suburban street, where an imposing copper front gate opens to reveal a 2-hectare tropical paradise set in a deep ravine blessed with volcanic soil and cooled by fountains and rivulets; it is a green antidote to the dry heat that pervades the island for many months of the year.

Several of Russell Page's golden rules of landscaping are evident at La Mortella or 'Place of Myrtles'. Susana Walton had a passion for trees and, if she'd had her own way, would have 'planted one of every tree in the

Opposite: A long rill runs between two pools and leads from the entrance of La Mortella into the heart of the Valley Garden, where water erupts from stone baths surrounded by lush tropical growth. 'Green fingers are an extension of a verdant heart,' wrote Russell Page in *The Education of a Gardener*.

world'. Page, however, advised planting by the hundreds, never using just single examples of any species. And he planted young trees, giving them a better chance of surviving winter gales. He also insisted on keeping the large rocks found throughout the property clear of vegetation to preserve their dramatic impact.

For the first three years of the garden's life, the soft, exotic plant species were protected by straw matting, which was strung across the valley. Today, orchids, billbergias and tillandsias cling to an ancient ginkgo, tulip trees, jacarandas and araucarias, which jostle with palms and swaths of tall tree ferns, the first of which—*Dicksonia antarctica*—was sent by William Walton in a shoe box from Australia, where he was conducting in 1965.

The ground is carpeted with bromeliads, flowering in red, yellow and orange spikes, which light up the dense green growth. Drifts of *Geranium maderense*, anthuriums and hostas flourish at the feet of heliconias flowering in brilliant hues.

Opposite, top: Higher parts of La Mortella's garden afford extraordinary views through wind-buffeted stone pines over the town of Forio and the blue waters of the Mediterranean. *Opposite, bottom*: Water is central to La Mortella. This fountain was designed by Russell Page for Sir William Walton's eightieth birthday. *Above*: The Victoria House, built to accommodate the revered *Victoria amazonica*, the largest water lily in the world. Orchids—cymbidiums, oncidiums, phalaenopsis and paphiopedilums—flourish in its humid environment, accompanied by the rare jade vine, *Strongylodon macrobotrys*.

Top, left to right: Bromeliads carpet the ground and cling to tree trunks at La Mortella. Here, *Guzmania* Samba, *Neoregelia* Myendorfii and Vriesea 'Carly'; *Coelogyne* Unchained Melody; *Odontocidium* Tiger Barb. ***Above:*** *Medinilla speciosa.* **Opposite:** A collection of tree ferns adds to the mysterious atmosphere of La Mortella's garden.

The Waltons built their home into the cliffside, looking over the garden and out to sea—today through a veil of exotic tropical creepers, including that great botanical diva, the jade vine (*Strongylodon macrobotrys*), native to the Philippines. There is also the Chilean jasmine (*Mandevilla laxa*), which produces glorious, scented white blooms in summer, and the delicate *Cobaea scandens*. A music studio and concert space were constructed on one of several terraces cut into the steep site and, in 2006, a Greek theatre was built for concerts that are held each weekend during the warm months.

On a high terrace a reservoir dubbed the Crocodile Pools is home to the Egyptian water lily (*Nymphaea caerulea*), no longer found in its north African habitat. Further on, the Temple of the Sun houses a collection of tropical palms, its walls adorned with carvings of Apollo, the god of music and poetry, by the English sculptor Simon Verity (b. 1946). Nearby, 'William's Rock' rests on the Belvedere; it is Lady Walton's memorial to her husband, who created such masterpieces as the lyric opera *Troilus and Cressida* at La Mortella.

More than half a century after their inception, these gardens continue to change and grow, fascinating thousands of garden-lovers each year. Lady Walton quotes Russell Page when she reminds me that 'a garden is an act of constant creation and renewal. It is never really finished.' You can believe this: 500 plants arrived the week I visited.

ARTISTS' GARDENS

RUSSELL PAGE

The English garden-maker Russell Page (1906–1985) considered himself first and foremost a gardener, rather than a designer or a landscape architect. Montague Russell Page was educated at Charterhouse and the University of London, and then studied painting in Paris, a passion that is seen in the pictures he created in the landscape.

He became a professional garden designer in 1928 and then worked, not only in England, but throughout much of Europe; he also designed gardens in the United States, and the Far East, including Sri Lanka. In 1946 he based himself in Paris.

'Processes have always given me more satisfaction than results,' he wrote. From the time it was published in 1962, his seminal book *The Education of a Gardener* has influenced generations of gardening men and women.

While his style was austere and somewhat restrained, when he added flowers to a garden, he did so in grand gestures. When asked if he was a plantsman or a designer, he responded, 'I know more about plants than most designers, and more about design than most plantsmen.'

La Casella

The cypress is always occupying my thoughts; it is as beautiful in line and proportion as an Egyptian obelisk, and the green has a quality of high distinction; it is a splash of black in a sunny landscape ...

VINCENT VAN GOGH (1853–1890) IN A LETTER TO HIS BROTHER
IN 1889, FROM ST REMY, PROVENCE

High in the hills behind Nice, in the south of France, La Casella shimmers in the late spring sunshine on the edge of the tiny village of Opio, near the perfumed town of Grasse. Overlooking the towns of the Côte d'Azur—but a world away from the frenetic rush of the coast—this is a garden written in the language of the heat and its light, and painted in greys, blues, lavenders and pinks, ochres and russets.

Created from 1984 by Tom Parr, a former director of the English design firm Colefax & Fowler, and by the landscaper Claus Scheinert, La Casella could only be located, one feels, in Provence.

This is difficult gardening country: in the rocky *garrigue*—the limestone soil of the south of France—only plants that can cope with hot summers and cold winters thrive. The steep slopes of the region are farmed in terraces—*restanques*—the traditional method of land management practised over many centuries, and home to vineyards and ancient plantings of olives.

At La Casella the house—roofed with the gently curved clay tiles typical of the region—is washed in a deep terracotta-pink and shaded by blue

Opposite: An almost-hidden entrance leads into the garden at La Casella: a gravel path winds past a series of clipped orbs of *Teucrium* and box in a variety of sizes. Pink-washed walls, olive trees and soaring cypress leave you in no doubt that you are in the Mediterranean.

shutters, perfect under the clear, brilliant light; a paler colour would look insipid. The house settles into the hillside and 2-hectare garden which, in tribute to the surrounding country-side, is terraced on several levels to create walkways, *allées* and axial points, vistas, and small, intimate enclosures. La Casella also bears witness to the design aesthetic that has created such a reputation for the firm of Colefax & Fowler: a restricted palette of colours is the refined canvas for dignified luxury.

Severely clipped evergreens, in silvers and greys and many shades of green, not only provide essential structure throughout the garden—so evident in the winter months when much of the garden is laid bare—but also a restful background and foil for walls and steps built in cool, well-weathered local stone. Orbs, tripods and cones—of teucrium, box, laurel and conifer—provide pleasing structure and give direction from one enclosed space to the next. Hedges are overlaid with luxuriant planting, a perfect foil for the froth of roses, wiste-rias and heavily scented jasmine that adorn the garden in spring and summer.

This is a garden with its back braced against the mountains, and high curtains of cypress provide essential protection from the infamous mistral wind, which can descend, wreaking havoc, at any time in summer.

Opposite, top: From this expansive terrace at the highest part of La Casella's garden, there are stunning views over the Provençal country-side. In spring, wisteria forms a scented canopy over a sturdy arbour, supported by up-scale stone columns. *Opposite, bottom*: A swath of agapanthus adds fascination over several weeks, from this early stage—so full of promise—to the full-blown spheres of blue stars, which open in midsummer. ***Above***: A circular, stone-edged pool in which a selection of Siberian iris and water lilies in blues and whites thrive. An intimate space has been created with hedges of conifer.

Above, left: Ancient olives, now sought at great expense by new gardeners in the region, lend presence to this restrained and calm section of La Casella's garden. *Above, centre*: Reaching 3 metres or more, spires of *Echium pininana* add height to the garden compartments. *Above, right*: Water, in various forms and shapes, is important at La Casella. *Opposite*: An arbour of roses and a hedge of lavender lead into another secret enclosure: gates cut into the cypress hedges provide access to an arbour of the frothy pink rose 'Madame Caroline Testout'. Windows in the dense green hedge provide enticing glimpses into gardens of roses and lavender.

A palette of plants that love the Mediterranean climate—hedges of conifers, edges of lavenders, and arches covered in blowsy roses in soft pinks and creams—reflect the Provençal vernacular. Plants that you might see on the dry hillsides also find a comfortable place in the gardens at La Casella: santolina, rosemary, lavender, thyme, box, cypress and laurel, the scent from their oils lingering in the hazy air. And the olive tree, with its twisted trunk and branches, and flickering, grey-green leaves, lends gravitas—and a clear sense of location—to the garden.

While the coastal Riviera and hinterland Provence quickly became cosmopolitan once discovered by American and British actors and writers in the late nineteenth and early twentieth centuries—'one of the enchanted landscapes of the human heart', according to English writer Lawrence Durrell—the region retains its own vernacular, in both architecture and garden design.

Berman Garden

The valley's full of misty clouds,
Its tinted beauty drowning,
Tree-tops are veiled in fleecy shrouds,
And mountain fronts are frowning.

The mist is hanging like a pall
Above the granite ledges,
And many a silvery waterfall
Leaps o'er the valley's edges.

HENRY LAWSON, 'RAIN IN THE MOUNTAINS', VERSES 1–2

The song of a thousand birds—feasting on the flowering eucalypts, banksias and persoonia that bloom in her Southern Highlands garden—wake the sculptor Bronwyn Berman each dawn. On misty mornings her house, which protrudes from a western escarpment of the Great Dividing Range, hundreds of metres above the Wingecarribee River, appears to be hovering above clouds.

Berman admits that the environment in which she lives and works—just west of the New South Wales country town of Bowral—can be overwhelming: there is always so much happening in the extraordinary landscape that surrounds the house, which was designed by the late architect Harry Seidler (1923–2006). As an artist she knows she could never improve on its beauty. She was inspired by the geography and geology of the landscape and its timeline, dating from Gondwana—the time when the land

Opposite, left to right: Bronwyn Berman's work is set among the indigenous flora in her garden; the broad-leafed drumstick, *Isopogon anemonifolius*; Bronwyn's sculpture, 'The Sphere', transforms rubble into a shape ever present in the landscape.

Top, left: The house in its garden of native species. *Top, centre:* 'The Journey', set under a canopy of the local stringybark, mimics the glass that is central to the house, and the patterns of life and the river below. The lower section, or canoe, is carved from a favourite tree that needed to be removed, and that Berman wanted to reinstate in the landscape. *Top, right:* 'The Wind Dragon' is suspended above a site that attracts fierce winds from the gorge below. The rocks around the work reflect the bend in the ancient river, where deposits of silt and pebbles were laid down long ago in pools and eddies. *Bottom:* The house floats above the escarpment and overlooks the river, from which the mists rise. Built of stone, steel and glass, its roofline rolls to reflect the mountains of this part of the Great Dividing Range folding out to the west. Just outside the front door is the mound garden, created from the local conglomerate, with its jewel-like quartz pebbles and chips of ironstone, in a palette of whites, greys, browns and blacks: the colours of the earth. The plant palette of sisyrinchiums and local grasses thrives in the tough conditions.

masses of what is now the southern hemisphere were fused to form one supercontinent—described by the escarpment. Her work is also influenced by 'the house and the scale of everything that is around: the creation, the landscape, the extremes of the wind'.

With an honours degree from the University of New South Wales' College of Fine Arts, Berman turned first to creating the garden after the disruption of the building, which took eight years from conception to completion. She felt a need to tidy up the garden—which runs to several hectares—and use the left-over building materials. The garden she has created blends seamlessly into its bush setting and employs species indigenous to the area. The drive into the property winds through local wattles that flower as a backdrop to *Banksia ericifolia*, with its inflorescences like glowing umber candles. In front, isopogons jostle with eriostemons, and the ground is carpeted with prostrate grevilleas and tiny brilliant blue harebells.

The local *Banksia serrata*—with its flowers and seedheads that inspired the frightening banksia men in *Snugglepot and Cuddlepie*, a series of children's books by Australian author May Gibbs (*see* below)—stands in the background, against huge sandstone rocks, over which the brilliant blue native wisteria *Hardenbergia violacea* scrambles.

Berman concedes the Australian bush is chaotic. Often using found materials—fencing wire, aluminium, stone and glass—her work seeks to understand her environment: 'so simplify, simplify. Spirals repeat: circles repeat.'

It is not surprising that Berman admits to 'spending a lot of time just looking, and being, and breathing in' her surroundings. This includes hours of contemplation over countless cups of tea.

MAY GIBBS

The Australian children's author May Gibbs (1877–1969) was best known for her series *Snugglepot and Cuddlepie*, which featured the terrifying banksia men and their victims, the charming gumnut babies, inspired by the spent flower heads of the eucalypts. Perhaps it is not surprising that some Australian gardeners have long disliked, or at best ignored, indigenous flora—after all, many middle-aged gardeners were raised on a literary diet of May Gibbs's gumnut babies and the villainous banksia men.

Cecelia May Gibbs was born in Sydenham, England; her family, which eventually included three brothers, moved to Australia in 1880. Gibbs studied art in London, but her most famous illustrations, inspired by the Australian bush, were not published until her return to the Sydney harbourside suburb of Neutral Bay in 1913. Her home there, Nutcote, is preserved as a museum to honour her work.

Bebeah

Bliss was it that dawn to be alive.

WORDSWORTH, *THE PRELUDE*, BK XI, LINE 108

Simply wandering the lanes that wind through the tiny hamlet of Mount Wilson, about 100 kilometres west of Sydney in the Blue Mountains, and peering over established hedges to gardens replete with century-old exotic trees, is exciting. During most months of the year log fires send swirling smoke into the cool mountain air, and mists can shroud the gardens in atmosphere. Often open to garden-lovers, these properties are both educational and inspirational.

Bebeah, a classic timber cottage with attic rooms and roofed with corrugated iron, was built in the 1880s for Edward Cox, a grazier from Rylstone, near Mudgee, a town a little further west, and the grandson of the pioneer William Cox. The house is now completely hidden from the road by 5 hectares of established gardens, beautifully restored by the designer Barry Byrne.

At the end of the long, gently curving drive you find a massive copper beech guarding the house; on the lawn to the other side of the house, the 30-metre spread of a century-old scarlet oak is now supported by stout poles. From the front of the house, which is decorated in spring with the yellow banksian rose, you cross a wide lawn to admire the first dogwood

Opposite: Pyramids of dwarf Alberta spruce (*Picea glauca* var. *albertiana* 'Conica') look so smart in front of Bebeah's timber cottage, tucked away in 5 hectares of magnificent established gardens. Beyond is the glorious copper beech that was planted when the house was built in the 1880s.

to be planted in Australia: it's a *Cornus florida* 'Rubra' and was imported from northern America in the nineteenth century. A long iron arbour leads to plantings of more than nine thousand azaleas, an extraordinary sight year round, but particularly in early October, when thousands of bluebells bloom at their feet.

Beyond the house an expansive lake, in which the spires of tall conifers are reflected, looks over the valley crowded with stands of *Cyathea australis,* the tree ferns indigenous to the area and a sign of an ancient garden; one created by nature. Hugging the banks of the lake are vignettes of clever planting; there is *Cotoneaster horizontalis* clambering over local rock, along with punctuation points of *Agave americana* 'Mediopicta' and spires of cream and yellow *Kniphofia* against the backdrop of mountain trees.

Further on, a stone bridge leads to a Barry Byrne folly, a temple which, with plantings of hundreds of rhododendron, is part of a grand plan that is the work of this artist and art historian, who has spent every day of the past decade in this garden. He advises that recognising when to stop with features is all-important, but admits, somewhat irreverently, that topiary is next on the agenda—whether rabbits or chickens, he's not sure.

Opposite, top: An American red oak shades a gravel path at Bebeah and banks of white-flowering azaleas are clipped into cloud hedges. *Opposite, bottom left*: Old stone steps lead through Japanese maples, azaleas and clipped spheres of gold conifers to a gate post salvaged from renovations to St Andrew's Anglican cathedral in Sydney. *Opposite, bottom right*: The slow-growing dwarf Alberta spruce (*Picea glauca* var. *albertiana* 'Conica') retains a beautiful conical shape. *Above*: Several terraces cut into the sloping site are retained by beautifully constructed drystone walls; planting is in broad sweeps. Here, a mass of prostrate juniper hugs a hand-thrown pot by Lino Alvarez.

GRAND PASSIONS

Obsessions are marvellous; grand passion an admirable quality. To pursue an ideal, relentlessly and energetically, is as exciting as it is all-consuming. The garden-makers in the following section have indulged their gardening passion with great vigour and, as a result, have created wonderful spaces. Such passion is uplifting, spiritual, nurturing, and emotionally and physically beneficial—even if at times exhausting.

Mount Stewart

Our England is a garden that is full of stately views,
Of borders, beds and shrubberies and lawns and avenues,
With statues on the terraces and peacocks strutting by;
But the Glory of the Garden lies in more than meets the eye.

RUDYARD KIPLING, 'THE GLORY OF THE GARDEN', VERSE 1

I would have loved to have met Edith, Marchioness of Londonderry (1878–1959). By all accounts she was a fabulous character, if perhaps a little daunting for those who could not quite match her in looks, position and spirit. She worked for women's rights and the suffragist movement, founded the Women's Legion and was an acclaimed hostess.

It is said she had a snake tattooed up her leg, so we might assume she was an original. And the garden she created around her home, Mount Stewart, in County Down, Northern Ireland, is also unique. It was created with the help of twenty ex-servicemen from World War I on a scale that would be inconceivable today. It remains a masterpiece of design and botanical importance.

Not far from Belfast, on the Ards Peninsula overlooking Strangford Lough, Mount Stewart is blessed with a benign, warm-temperate climate, courtesy of the Gulf Stream. The stone house dates from the early nineteenth century—Robert Stewart, 1st Marquess of Londonderry, influenced by his grand tour of Europe, implemented plans drawn up by London architect George Dance, a founding member of the Royal Academy in

Opposite: At Mount Stewart, one of Ireland's most celebrated gardens: looking from the Dodo Terrace towards the southern face of the stone house, and across the Italian Garden, which is some 30 metres long by 17 metres wide, and encloses a series of parterres.

1768 and Professor of Architecture between 1798 and 1805. The Georgian house was enlarged as successive generations increased their wealth and political importance, but was described by Edith, after her arrival there in 1919, as 'the darkest, dampest, saddest place I ever stayed in'. Under her direction, however, Mount Stewart became famous for its glittering receptions for politicians of all persuasions, artists and writers. And for its gardens, inspired by her travels to the best in Italy: among them the Palazzo Farnese, Villa Gamberaia and Boboli Gardens. She corresponded with the plant hunters of the period and commissioned designs from English plantswoman and garden designer Gertrude Jekyll (1843–1932).

Today the gardens are maintained by seven full-time gardeners, with the benefit of Edith's meticulously detailed garden diaries and extensive plant lists.

Opposite, top: The walk around Mount Stewart's lake leads through horticultural treasures from South America, China, New Zealand and Australia. *Opposite, bottom left*: The delicate Mairi Fountain, modelled on his daughter, was designed by Lord Londonderry. *Opposite, bottom centre*: Edith Londonderry's sense of humour: animals on plinths, each representing a politician friend, on the Dodo Terrace. *Opposite, bottom right*: One of the gallery of amusing animals that represented Edith's famous friends. *Above*: The south-facing Italian Garden, which runs the length of the house.

The Sunken Garden, folding out from the western face of the house, was created from a design sent by Jekyll and is embraced by an up-scale pergola covered in honeysuckle and climbing roses, including the golden *R*. 'Lady Hillingdon', 'Lawrence Johnston' and 'Mai-gold'. Hedges of traditional, deep green yew (*Taxus baccata*), a coathanger for the climbing, red-flowered nasturtium (*Tropaeolum speciosum*), enclose this generous space, creating one of several compartments that have resulted in the microclimate that has contributed so significantly to the success of Mount Stewart. Four black-leaved *Acer* 'Crimson King' stand, in stone planters, at the entrances to this section of the garden, which also houses Edith's beloved delphiniums.

Further on in the Shamrock Garden, a yew is clipped into the shape of an Irish harp, and is underplanted with oxalis. The red hand of Ulster, bedded out annually in a seasonal variety of crimson plants—begonias, impatiens or salvias, often preceded by red tulips—is among several motifs alluding to Ireland's history. The Lily Wood leads to the Spanish Garden, with its rills, mature tree peonies and twisted, standard wisterias, designed by Edith to be seen from the house and afford views across the sea to the distant Mountains of Morn. Close by is the Dodo Terrace, shaded by stands of *Eucalyptus globulus*; here Edith's quirky sense of humour is given voice: stone animals recall what she called her Ark Club, when visiting luminaries, including Winston Churchill, were given the names of birds, beasts or mythical creatures.

The Italian Garden, influenced by Edith's visit to the Villa Gamberaia in Tuscany—with its several 'rooms' tied together by a 240-metre grass *allée*—runs the full length of the south side of the house. A parterre of beds, edged in berberis, heather and holly—for she disliked box—constrains a colour scheme that travels from the sunset colours of dahlias, cannas, day lilies and kniphofias to the cool blues and pinks of delphiniums and salvias. These summer beds reach their best during August, and continue to perform until early winter, when structure becomes the star.

September is perhaps the best time to walk around the 4-hectare lake, where the autumn leaves on a fascinating collection of trees are reflected in still waters. Many, including the tender, gloriously scented *Rhododendron lindleyi* and *R. fragrantissimum*, have been grown from seed collected on the expeditions of plant hunters Frank Kingdon-Ward, George Forrest and Joseph Rock, whom Edith sponsored and with whom she corresponded. There is a group of *Acer cappadocicum*, the honey-scented *Weinmannia trichosperma* from New Zealand, Tasmanian beech, monkey puzzle trees, cordylines, and the palm-like Australian *Richea dracophylla*. With the walk of bamboo—including *Himalayacalamus falconeri* and *Phyllostachys* spp.—they provide the feel of a high country garden of the Indian subcontinent.

There is a great deal more at Mount Stewart, including the delightful Mairi Garden, with its exquisite, delicate fountain, and the Ladies' Walk, alluding to a time when gardens were laid out as parklands, some distance from the house, for promenading.

Northern Ireland is home to several important and exciting gardens. Mount Stewart is one.

Top: Mount Stewart's Spanish Garden—so called because the summer-house is roofed with green tiles—is enclosed by hedges of × *Cupressocyparis leylandii* to shelter collections of peonies, wisterias, viburnums and rhododendrons. ***Bottom:*** The Sunken Garden is embraced by a rose-covered pergola and leads to the Shamrock Garden, where a yew is clipped into the shape of an Irish harp.

Ilnacullin

When rosy May comes in wi' flowers
To deck her gay, green, spreading bowers;
Then busy, busy are his hours,
The gardener wi' his paidle.

The crystal waters gently fa';
The merry birds are lovers a';
The scented breezes round him blaw,
The gardener wi' his paidle.

ROBERT BURNS, 'THE GARDENER'S MARCH', VERSES 1–2

May is the month to visit Ilnacullin's garden, if it is the collection of rhodo-dendrons you want to see. It is then that the delicious scent of *R. arbores-cens*, native to the United States, fills the garden. The very fragrant hybrid *R.* 'Lady Alice Fitzwilliam', parading pale pink to cream flowers marked with yellow, is also in bloom. There is *R. sinogrande*, from China and Myan-mar (formerly Burma) which, in this sheltered environment, grows almost to its natural 15 metres and bears massive, leathery foliage and balls of cream to yellow blooms. It provides shaded protection for the Himalayan *R. thomsonii*, sporting its marvellous peeling bark. The tall-growing, yellow-flowered *R. maccabeanum* is native to India, while *R. yakushimanum* is native to Japan and coveted for its trusses of cream bells and protective, felty indumentum that coats the undersides of its leaves.

Opposite: Glorious views across the gardens are afforded from the Martello Tower, at a high point at Ilnacullin. The Clock Tower—in a corner of the Walled Garden—and the Pavilion are visible, before you look across the water to the rugged, heather-covered Caha Mountains, which form a spectacular backdrop to the gardens.

One way to find Ilnacullin is to take the beautiful Pass of Keimaneigh west of Cork and descend precariously, but triumphantly, between the mountains that run between Ballingarry and Ballylicky on the coast. Ilnacullin garden covers the 15-hectare Garinish Island, which rests in an idyllic cove in glistening Bantry Bay, the world's deepest harbour, in south-west Ireland's County Cork. A ferry to the island is caught from Glengarriff, the fishing village set on one of the countless inlets that slice into this rocky shore. Seals bask on craggy outcrops that bear stands of deep green conifers.

Like much of Scotland, England and Ireland, this wild and beautiful coastline is washed by the warm Gulf Stream, making it possible to create large gardens to showcase the botanical bounty brought from the colonial outposts on the Indian subcontinent by intrepid nineteenth-century plant hunters.

Ilnacullin, which means 'Island of Holly', was the magnificent obsession of John Annan Bryce, a Belfast-born member of parliament, who bought the exposed, inhospitable island in 1910 from the British War Office. With some help from the English architect and landscaper Harold Peto (1854–1933), and assisted by an annual rainfall of some 1850 millimetres, Bryce created a renowned garden of rare plants from around the world.

Shelter belts of Scots pine were immediately planted to create a microclimate and protection from the Atlantic winds. Soil was brought from the mainland to lay over the existing

Opposite, top: The Casita, or Tea House—the centrepiece of Ilnacullin's Italian Garden—is set again the background of the craggy Caha Mountains. *Opposite, bottom:* Several of Garinish Island's rocks are used to good effect in the garden: they are left exposed, hosting rambling roses like 'American Pillar'. ***Above:*** Rocky outcrops and mist-covered mountains are the theatrical backdrop to this exhilarating garden.

grey shale, although many granite rocks were retained, exposed as features throughout the garden. The deep pink rose 'American Pillar' scrambles over a large, weather-beaten rock; meticulously pruned, it becomes one mass of colour in late June to mid July. Another rock is covered in a mix of the cerise-to-blue-flowering climber 'Veilchenblau', along with 'Chaplin's Pink Climber' and the deep pink 'Zéphirine Drouhin'.

The rhododendrons of May are followed by wisteria, which blooms in early June in curtains of scented lilac over a mellow stone pavilion, La Casita—the centrepiece of the Italian Garden. The rugged and romantic Caha Mountains of County Cork and Kerry, which provide such a sense of place to this garden, erupt, glowering, in the background.

From the Italian Garden, weathered stone stairs climb to the Temple of the Winds, which frames spectacular views of the Sugar Loaf and Hungry Hill mountains, part of the Caha Mountains. From there, a glade of rhododendron leads to the Martello Tower, one of many such fortifications built around the Irish coast in the early nineteenth century to guard against a feared Napoleonic invasion. This spot has the best views into the Walled Garden and across the water to surrounding islands.

John Annan Bryce made his fortune from Russia's oil and teak, only to lose it during the 1917 revolution; as a result, a two-room cottage was built instead of the Peto design for a grand, seven-story residence. In 1923, encouraged by friends, Annan Bryce decided to open his gardens to the public to supplement his budget. He died later that year, and his widow, Violet, continued the garden, which was gifted to the Irish people when her son Roland died in 1953. Today these marvellous gardens are maintained by the Office of Public Works and by seven full-time gardeners.

If the deep pink rose 'Bantry Bay'—which also comes as a lovely climber—is named after this spot, you'll want it in your garden to remind you of this beautiful corner of Ireland. Today more than 100 000 visitors enjoy Ilnacullin annually, but the garden still imparts the romantic, private and secluded feeling that must have filled Annan Bryce and his wife with such excitement and passion.

Coton Manor

The snowdrop, and then the violet,
Arose from the ground with warm rain wet,
And their breath was mixed with fresh odour, sent
From the turf, like the voice and the instrument.

PERCY BYSSHE SHELLEY, *THE SENSITIVE PLANT,* **VERSE 4**

Susie Pasley-Tyler insists that it is her mother-in-law who should be cred-
ited with the masterful planting in her Northhamptonshire garden, Coton
Manor, while she says her father-in-law is to be congratulated on its design.
With her husband, Ian, Susie now gardens in 5 hectares of what must be
English perfection, having taken over from Ian's parents in 1992.

Coton Manor also benefits from its setting, sited in a south-westerly
position looking out across a sylvan countryside. To Susie it is 'more English than anything else you'll find … slightly rolling, very understated, but
very beautiful'.

There is something in this garden to fascinate virtually year round—the
complicated terrace borders, arranged to harness the sloping site, change
in theme, texture and tone as spring moves into summer, then autumn,
and beyond. Susie has to think on many different dimensions in terms of
time and manages each border so that it comes into its own as the one
above is slightly off its best: they don't all peak at the same time. As most
of the borders are extensive; large blocks of successful plants are repeated
to engender a sense of rhythm and unity.

An advocate of the 'less is more' theory, Susie has designed each border
around a different but disciplined colour palette: she believes an area limited to just a few colours is much more effective. In gardening, she has
discovered a latent talent for playing with colour.

Opposite: Stone steps lead through the woodland past water-loving species to
the lower rose gardens and on to the wild meadow and bluebell woods.

A collection of alpine species is the first to perform in the garden. It is laid out on the terrace of local stone on which the house—which has been extended from its seventeenth-century core—rests. As the alpines finish, the main borders come into flower. The south-facing walls of the house provide the perfect canvas for an espaliered flannel bush (*Fremontodendron californicum*), a golden wedding anniversary present to Ian's parents, along with cascades of wisteria, clematis and climbing roses, which flower over several months to ensure a continuous curtain of colour and scent.

As you walk around the terrace you come to the rose garden, which is a mass of pink and white roses bred by the Reverend Pemberton, as well as the early David Austin–bred roses, such as the medium-sized 'Mary Rose'. They flower in clouds of soft pink and white, accompanying the pink herbaceous *Paeonia* 'Sarah Bernhardt' and white *P. lactiflora* 'Duchess de Nemours'. In this 'garden room', plants that would otherwise be swamped in the rest of the garden and which flower before the roses receive a chance to star. As soon as the roses have bloomed, Susie cuts them back. The rose garden is flanked on one side by an ancient hedge of holly, which provides the backdrop to the main border.

This border peaks at the end of May and includes touches of red—stunning against the holly hedge—as well as many blue-flowering plants and 'a certain amount of white'. There are four large clumps of the red *Penstemon* 'Garnet', teamed with the red *Salvia microphylla* and *S. involucrata* 'Bethellii'. Once the tulips in this border are finished, they will be replaced in the

Opposite, top: The stone house around which Coton Manor's garden is set was built in 1662 and is covered in wisteria and the old rose 'Seven Sisters', which displays several shades of pink and blooms in trusses of up to seven flowers. *Opposite, bottom left*: The Holly Border is an example of the changing themes and colours of each season. In early spring silvers, greys and yellows dominate, moving to deep blues and scarlets in high summer, and a dominance of white and cream in autumn. The fascinating and biblical *Dictamnus albus*, with its fragrant flower, is teamed with alliums, species geraniums and roses. *Opposite, bottom right*: The tulip 'Queen of the Night' is planted in the dark border with a purple-leaved *Dicentra* and *Penstemon digitalis* 'Husker Red'. *Above*: The main border employs a framework of roses, peonies, dahlias, euphorbias, sedums and the frothy, early-flowering *Thalictrum aquilegiifolium*, within which a repetition of selected plants provides constant drama.

Top: Coton Manor's herb garden, the size of a tennis court, is yet another lesson in good design. Behind a screen of espaliered apples are six circular beds, edged in miniature box; in the centre are two arrowhead-shaped beds. Hedges of yew provide a perfect foil for screens covered in sweet peas and runner beans. *Centre, left to right:* Tellimas, ligularias and alliums thrive in the water gardens.
Bottom: Thousands of garden-lovers flock each May to the 2-hectare woodland of English bluebells at the base of the gardens at Coton Manor. Carpeting the ground beneath hundreds of beech trees, the azure blooms contrast brilliantly with the fresh lime green of the new spring leaves.

first week of May with *Dahlia sherffii*, blooming with clutches of delphiniums. To add height, eight groups of phlox are planted with a deep indigo agapanthus. The white bells of *Galtonia candicans* appear in August with white agapanthus to freshen up the border in midsummer. Cones and tee-pees, created from hazelnut prunings, support peonies, roses and clematis and contribute a third dimension to the scheme, while grey-foliaged species, planted throughout, tie it all together. This main border is cut back in both July and at the end of the flowering season; in November it is pruned ruthlessly and mulched with cow manure and compost.

An inviting gate at the far end of the wide grass terrace, cut into a well-established yew hedge, leads to the woodland garden—at its peak in April, but full of quiet greens through summer—and on to the water and stream gardens. Excitement mounts, yet again, at the wealth and combinations of plant material, many planted decades ago.

In the water gardens, swaths of a pinky-orange-flowered form of *Primula japonica* and the aristocratic *Kirengeshoma palmata* hug the edges of a spring-fed stream, illuminated by the lovely heart's tongue fern. The purple-leaved corydalis complements *Tellima grandiflora* 'Rubra'; *Allium aflatunense* 'Purple Sensation' is planted with *Ligularia dentata* 'Desdemona'. The feathery flowers of *Astilbe* 'Bressingham Beauty' look marvelous with *Rodgersia pinnata* 'Superba', *Astrantia* 'Margery Fish' and *Saxifraga fortunei* 'Wada's Variety', with its frilly white blooms in autumn; the latter is a favourite of Susie's as it is understated but enjoys a prolonged flowering.

Towards the bottom of the garden is the largest double border, at its height in midsummer, thereby peaking slightly later than the border by the holly hedge. When in full throttle, it is bursting with deep pinks and purples, set off with a bit of yellow. Susie prefers this border earlier, however, when it is more sedate. Among the prima donnas here is *Ligularia przewalskii*, punctuated by tripods of roses and clematis. The prized poppy 'Patty's Plum' is planted with bronze fennel, the purple-leaved smoke bush *Cotinus* 'Grace', the rugosa rose 'Belle Poitevine', as well as the cerise Bourbon rose 'Madame Isaac Pereire'. Close by in the rose walk, reds and pinks turn into creams and golds: a tripod of the rose 'Maigold' is planted with a honeysuckle 'Dropmore Scarlet', which is less rampant than most, and is highlighted with a flash of red from the climbing nasturtium, *Tropaeolum speciosum*.

In the wild meadow, tens of thousands of spring bulbs have naturalised with primroses, ox-eye daisies, campions and other wildflowers.

While admitting that gardening is her passion, Susie denies she is a plantswoman. Her interest lies more in composition, finding 'the right habitat for things'. For her, gardening lies somewhere in the middle—between plantspeople and garden designers.

However, passionate gardeners are the same the world over, it seems. Susie admits that she adores the genus *Meconopsis*, which includes the coveted Himalayan blue poppy. She works to get the drainage of the garden correct and the soil 'just on the acid side of neutral [to] grow meconopsis ... they don't naturalise'. To Susie garden-making is 'the most enthralling thing. Completely absorbing.'

Yarrawa

Come rainbow or the rose,
Vision shall find new birth:
With love more lovely grows
Beauty on earth.

T INGLIS MOORE, 'SONG FOR LOVERS', VERSE 4

When Bruce Rosenberg bought his property in the Southern Highlands of New South Wales in 1993, the area had been cleared of its indigenous rainforest of blackwood, coachwood, cedar, sassafras, lilypilly and the giant brown barrel, *Eucalyptus fastigata*. Known as Yarrawa Brush, the rainforest remained pristine, apart from the felling of native cedars by timber cutters, until the *Robertson Land Act* 1861: the area was then logged and cleared for agriculture, denuding it of the old-growth forest.

Bruce wanted to reinstate something of the original rainforest at the entrance to his property, which he called Yarrawa. This would also provide privacy and protection from the south-westerly winds. The trees, planted as tube stock, are now well established, thanks to deep chocolate-cake-rich volcanic soil, a rainfall of some 1500 millimetres per year and judicious planting of short-lived, fast-growing wattles to act as protective 'nurse plants'.

Opposite: A rainforest of species, all indigenous to this eastern side of the Southern Highlands in New South Wales, forms a mysterious, but welcoming, entrance to Yarrawa. Once inside the garden proper, a landscape of enclosed 'rooms' teams with generous expanses and scaled-up plantings to create an impressive whole.

Influenced by the gardens of the Italian Renaissance—with their emphasis on the importance of scale and size, their disciplined use of natural materials and of a restricted palette of plant species—Bruce Rosenberg has created a garden that is an excellent lesson in good design. He is another follower of the less-is-more theory and has limited the number of different plants in his 2-hectare garden. Large beds, and generous plantings, are at home here. The wide curves facilitate mowing and, apart from a few trees in lawns for strategic reasons, most are planted in copses with rough grass occasionally mown underneath. And, with the bonus of a borrowed landscape of rolling dairy country, the success of this garden is quickly obvious.

Opposite, top: Yarrawa's house sits snugly in its undulating garden against a backdrop of the local brown barrel, *Eucalyptus fastigata*. The yellow flag iris (*Iris pseudacorus*) and giant rhubarb (*Gunnera manicata*) erupt each spring by the lake. *Opposite, bottom left:* Everything here, including pergolas, is 'scaled up'. *Opposite, bottom centre: Euphorbia characias* subsp. *wulfennii. Opposite, bottom right:* A work in steel by Phocion Vouros depicts the Athenian Lysistrata, a woman who, in the Aristophanes play of 411 BC, helped end the Peloponnesian War. *Above:* The house overlooks the lake and rolling dairy country—often shrouded in mist, even in summer.

Above: Paths wind through woodlands of viburnums, dogwoods, maples and birches. Underplantings are of massed *Ajuga*, several species of hellebores, iris and the small periwinkle, *Vinca minor*. Spring-flowering daffodils and jonquils are also favourites. Hedges are of *Escallonia bifida* and viburnums. *Opposite, top:* The hellebore walk. *Opposite, bottom left:* Rocks from the basalt soil provide for stone walling and a pyramid built at the end of a grass walk. It is flanked by clipped orbs of western red cedar, *Thuja plicata*. *Opposite, bottom right:* Celeste Coucke's work in lead and steel, *Colonisation*, pays tribute to indigenous reconciliation.

Once past the rainforest entrance, several superb areas open out, with breathtaking views over the surrounding green hills. In the first garden section, beneath a canopy of trees related to those in the rainforest, a massive sweep of plant material is home to a scaled-up urn. There, the collection of hydrangeas includes most of the species: the shade-loving macrophyllas, plus the quercifolias, paniculatas and serratas, which can take more sun. As several of each species were bought, a full and voluminous effect was quickly achieved.

There is *Hydrangea arborescens*, with arresting, lime green mopheads. *Hydrangea aspera* var. *villosa* makes a large statement with mauve lacecap flowers at the back of a border, and the long-flowering quercifolias have rich, wine-coloured leaves in autumn. The climbing variety, *H. anomala* subsp. *petiolaris*, looks very effective as ground cover after Bruce saw it so employed at Kew Gardens, London.

Yarrawa is a glorious garden that employs lessons in scale and size, restraint in choice of plant material, the magic of location, along with passion, to great effect.

Larnach Castle

*I wonder if I shall fall right through
the earth! How funny it'll seem
to come out among people that walk with
their heads downwards! The antipathies, I think ...*

LEWIS CARROLL, *ALICE'S ADVENTURES IN WONDERLAND*, MACMILLAN & CO., LONDON, 1865

We all know that young people do impetuous things; that actions sometimes take place before careful planning. It doesn't get much more spontaneous than arriving in a kombivan on holidays, pregnant with your first child, at a rundown castle—and buying it.

That's what Margaret Barker did in 1967, when she bought Larnach Castle near Dunedin on New Zealand's south island. A Victorian pile comprising thirty-five rooms, its half-hectare roof leaked over intricate ceilings and woodwork carved from mahogany, blackwood, ebony and native honeysuckle. Its 18 hectares of garden and woodland were also in a sad state of neglect.

The castle, built from 1871 by William Larnach—an Australian merchant, land speculator and politician who arrived in the country around 1867—housed a turbulent and tragic history. In an extraordinary story of courage, vision and seemingly boundless energy, Margaret has restored the castle and its grounds. Today, the once-abandoned gardens that encroached upon the castle walls showcase treasures from the Pacific, Asia and the Indian subcontinent, as well as from the northern hemisphere.

Opposite: Views from the new South Seas Garden at Larnach Castle extend across Otago Peninsula and the harbour and on to the Pacific Ocean. This newly planted section of the garden houses rare and endangered species, along with others that cope with the exposed conditions.

The first task after the purchase was completed—beyond the massive restoration of the castle—was to clear some of the ancient pines, which had reached their senescence, to open up wonderful views across the Otago Peninsula and its harbour, and out to the Pacific Ocean. Now, a laburnum walk leads the visitor across the lawns that roll out in front of the house towards vistas cut through stands of *Pinus macrocarpa,* thus connecting the garden to the sea beyond.

Close to the house is the English Garden, an intimate space created around a serpentine path, and enclosed by a hedge of different species of holly. Its purpose is to slow people down to look at flowers from different aspects and angles. Margaret explains that the 'colour spectrum crosses your vision'.

Behind the house, tall New Zealand tree ferns shade a collection of rhododendrons, including the scented, white 'Stead's Best'—a local cross between *R. lindleyi* and *R. nuttali.* There is also the deep red *R. facetum* to offset a planting of the pink-and-teale-foliaged *Phormium* 'Tricolor'.

The terraced South Seas Garden, created in the late 1990s on a steep slope looking out to the ocean, houses species that cope with the salt winds that assault the site, while paying tribute to this wonderful location.

Opposite, top: Larnach Castle's collection of succulents includes the endangered *Aloe polyphylla* with its whirling growth pattern and orange flowers, growing alongside *Agave ferox. Opposite, bottom*: The exposed South Seas Garden survives salt-laden winds. *Aciphylla glaucescens* and the acid-yellow flowers of *Aeonium undulatum* usher you into this area. *Top, left*: *Phormium tenax*, from the nearby Chatham Islands, is used to make the traditional Maori baskets known as *keti*: this one, resting among the flax in the South Seas Garden, is created in steel by Maori artist Joe Kake. *Top, centre*: The grass, *Festuca coxii*, also from the Chatham Islands, softens a ceramic work by local artist Jenny Spiegal. *Top, right*: The laburnum walk. *Above*: Mass plantings of scented mollis azaleas create a terrace between the house and front lawns.

PRIVATE PLEASURES

For most of us our garden is a private sanctuary—a place to play and experiment or indulge our creative whims. It is often a personal struggle to create the beauty that is essential in our lives.

Hodges Barn

... and the woodbine spices are wafted abroad,
and the musk of the roses blown.

For a breeze of morning moves,
And the planet of Love is on high,
Beginning to faint in the light that she loves
On a bed of daffodil sky ...

ALFRED, LORD TENNYSON, *MAUD,* **XXII, LINES 5–10**

The extraordinarily beautiful garden at Hodges Barn is set in the midst of Gloucestershire, a picture postcard county not far from London.

An 8-hectare garden, Hodges Barn was laid out many decades ago around a pretty house, which was once a pair of domed dovecotes. Built in 1499 of Cotswold stone, they were converted into a home in 1938. Beautiful walls and hedges enclosing and defining spaces, wonderfully trained roses of all descriptions, and highly skilled planting schemes are features of this intensely exciting garden.

A wide lawn, bound by a rose-covered wall, leads to the façade of the house, which supports a dramatic mix of roses: there is the very red rose 'Danse du Feu', as well as 'Paul's Himalayan Musk', 'Wedding Day', 'Francis E Lester' and 'Rambling Rector'. There are also the yellow roses 'Gloire de Dijon' and 'Maigold'. In the wide stone steps that lead to the front door, potentillas, violets and tiny species geraniums have made themselves at home.

Opposite: Built of Cotswold stone, Hodges Barn was once a pair of domed dovecotes, until some seventy years ago when it was converted into its present form. It is now at the centre of a glorious Gloucestershire garden of old roses, clematis, deep perennial borders, woodland and wild meadow.

Mown paths, which meander through a wild garden of Queen Anne's lace and buttercups, lead beyond the formal gardens, to cool, shady woodland glades of magnolias, copper beech, dogwoods, horse chestnuts and maples. In this area, wild species roses, including the American *R. nutkana*—with its single, lilac-pink bloom—and the apple rose (*R. villosa*, syn. *R. pomifera*), clamber up trees and carpet the ground. A tapestry hedge of the common beech (*Fagus sylvatica*) and its purple offspring *F. sylvatica* 'Purpurea' directs the visitor back into the formal areas.

There, a vegetable garden and herb garden adjacent to the tennis court are divided into sections edged with box hedges, with one section given over to the picking garden. At one end of the swimming pool, which is enclosed by hedges of yew, is a burgundy border of *Rosa glauca*, with its thornless, purple shoots, and the crimson-leaved, but thorny, *Berberis thunbergii* 'Atropurpurea'. On the other side is an orchard of fruit trees growing in a romantic meadow of roughly mown grass.

From the swimming pool, a walk through an avenue of yew (*Taxus baccata*) provides enticing glimpses of a distant stone urn. A series of hedges of beech and cypress leads back

Opposite, top: Lawns roll out in front of Hodges Barn, its mellow walls providing a canvas for climbing roses and honeysuckle. *Opposite, bottom:* Deep borders are bursting with old-fashioned roses, species geraniums and hostas. Plantings of the purple-leaved *Berberis* add structure and break up the space into workable sections. *Above:* An avenue of yew (*Taxus baccata*) leads to a stone urn, which is set against a backdrop of hedges in beech and cypress.

Top: Wild species roses—including the large, arching and fragrant American *R. nutkana*—ramble through the wild garden at Hodges Barn. The blooms are followed by oval red hips. ***Above, left to right:*** *R.* 'Danse de Feu', sometimes called 'Spectacular', is a climber bred in France in 1953; *R.* 'Tuscany Superb'; *R.* 'Wedding Day'. *Opposite:* The swimming pool walls provide a home for fruit trees and roses, such as *Rosa glauca*, with its thornless, purple shoots, grey leaves and soft pink blooms.

towards the house, through more stone walls, which are 'finished off' with stone-carved pine cones. Topiary yew doves guard a grass terrace graced by a pair of the rare crabapple *Malus transitoria* from China and East Asia.

A lower grass terrace is simply planted with four superb magnolias, one marking each corner. This gives way to a deep perennial border, which hugs the gravelled area surrounding the northern side of the house. This pink and burgundy border is replete with dianthus, potentillas, the blue-flowered *Geranium × magnificum*, *Rosa rugosa* 'Scabrosa' and the single-flowered *R. glauca* (syn. *R. rubrifolia*), particularly lovely when the light illuminates her grey leaves. This combination is stunning, set against the cerise hues of berberis.

A winding path then leads back to a semi-circular hedge of beech, which forms the resting place for the urn spotted earlier.

Lismore Castle

Art beats nature altogether here.

CHARLES DARWIN (1809–1882), SPEAKING OF SIR JOSEPH PAXTON'S GREAT
CONSERVATORY, BUILT AT CHATSWORTH HOUSE BETWEEN 1836 AND 1841

You come upon spectacular Lismore Castle almost by surprise, as you round a bend on the N72, which snakes along the Blackwater, the river that runs through the charming old town from which the castle takes its name—not far from Waterford in Ireland's south.

The twelfth-century castle, on the site of a seventh-century monastery, has been a bishop's palace and the home of English explorer Sir Walter Raleigh, has withstood a sacking during the Cromwellian wars, played host to politicians, kings and queens and, for more than four centuries, has been the Irish seat of the Duke of Devonshire.

This 400-year-old garden is one of the few surviving Jacobean gardens in the United Kingdom and Ireland and has been continuously cultivated since it was laid out by the Great Earl of Cork in 1620. It is worth braving every twist and turn along the sometimes baffling Irish road system to see it.

The 4-hectare main garden is divided into upper and lower areas, each arranged as a series of expansive terraces. The summer garden is laid out on the upper level, against the austere backdrop of turreted walls, almost

Opposite: A high terrace at the twelfth-century Lismore Castle provides a bird's-eye view of the glorious parterre gardens. The 4-hectare main garden is terraced into upper and lower areas, arranged against the background of the castle, its thick walls playing host to climbing roses. The terraces are divided by deep green yew hedges into manageable compartments. Grass paths, edged with lavender, lead past voluptuous flowering borders in a series of colourways, from cool hues, through to sunset shades. A central axis is aligned with the distant spire of the town's Anglican cathedral.

a metre thick and 4 metres high and which still bear the marks of Cromwell's onslaught. Today they are only called upon to support cascades of the golden climbing tea rose 'Lady Hillingdon'.

Yew hedges break up the space, creating a large-scale parterre, with a central axis aligned to the distant spire of the town's Anglican cathedral. Grass paths lead past voluptuous flowering borders backed by hedges of forest-green: buttresses of yew divide the borders into manageable areas. The hot border showcases the red *Dahlia* 'Bishop of Llandaff', teamed with the copper-coloured bearded iris 'Kent Pride'; it is cooled by the blue perennial *Clematis integrifolia,* which clambers over a sturdy tripod. Tall blue spires of delphiniums are backed with the clear red of the climbing nasturtium *Tropaeolum speciosum,* which weaves through the deep green yew. Progressing along the border, the colours change to the burgundies of the purple-leaved smoke bush (*Cotinus* 'Purpureus'), the purple-leaved hazelnut and the purple-leaved canna, backdrops to the cerise-flowering *Knautia macedonica* and a hot pink peony. Then come the pinks and yellows, until finally the border ends calmly in creams and whites.

On the middle terrace, rows of potatoes are lined with white geraniums, to enliven a solid block of green. The hydrangea border, backed again by clipped yew hedges, is laid out on

Opposite, top: The twelfth-century Lismore Castle rises majestically above the green fields that hug the Blackwater River in the town of Lismore, southern Ireland. At the centre of a wonderful, 400-year-old garden, the spectacular castle has been the Irish home of the Dukes of Devonshire since 1753. *Opposite, bottom left*: The lower section of the garden is home to much of Lismore Castle's important collection of sculpture. Here, 'Over and Under' by the Irish artist Ellis O'Connell. *Opposite, bottom right*: A quiet seat is surrounded by the modern climbing rose 'Dublin Bay'. *Above:* The upper terrace, with its buttresses of clipped yew, houses part of Lismore Castle's collection of sculptures by contemporary artists.

Above: Joseph Paxton's vinery greenhouses, at the north-western end of Lismore Castle's upper garden, were built in the nineteenth century; each variety of vines has its own glass roof, which opens separately according to the variety's individual needs. *Opposite:* The lower section of the grounds is dominated by species loved by the 6th Duke of Devonshire, including a marvellous collection of magnolias. In the spring garden, a vaulted walkway of yew is more than four centuries old; it was once a Bishops' walkway to any of the seven churches in the town, and today houses more of the castle's collection of sculpture.

the third terrace. A range of hydrangeas, including the large-flowered mopheads, the oak-leaved species, *Hydrangea quercifolia*, and the frothy lacecaps are shaded by a collection of the Australian bottlebrush—very fashionable in European gardens.

Joseph Paxton, the nineteenth-century head gardener at Chatsworth House (the Duke of Devonshire's Derbyshire estate), who was later knighted for his design of London's Crystal Palace, built the innovative vinery greenhouses at the north-western end of the upper garden; each of a variety of vines has its own glass roof, which opens individually according to each plant's needs. The adjoining orchard houses a rare selection of old Irish varieties of apple trees, so important in Celtic times: in late winter they are carpeted with daffodils, followed by tulips and, in summer, lupins in a kaleidoscope of colour.

In the lower section of the grounds, the spring garden is dominated by a vaulted walkway of 450-year-old yew; it was once a bishop's walkway to any of the seven churches in the town. In May, the collection of magnolias is in flower, including the coveted *M. campbellii* and the rare *M. hypoleuca*, with its cream, heavily scented spring and summer flowers. And this is where a huge collection of rhododendrons, camellias and azaleas blooms from winter through to early summer.

As you somewhat reluctantly leave these wonderful grounds, the castle, seeming to stretch forever, towers over you as you head out of the village on the way to another beautiful Irish garden.

Jack's Ridge

Flowers of red silk and purple velvet grew
under the humming may-tree; the huge pines
made night across the grass, where the black snake
went whispering in its coil; and moving sunlight drew
copper fingers through the apple-trees.
Warm is the light the summer day refines ...

JUDITH WRIGHT, 'THE GARDEN', VERSE 1

Discipline and restraint have combined with vitality and clever plantsmanship to make Jack's Ridge one of Australia's most exciting gardens.
Home to Susan and Graeme Jack, this lovely garden, set on Victoria's Morn-
ington Peninsula, looks good through each of the year's four seasons.

In spring and summer, roses blend with wisterias, lavenders and mass
plantings of blue and white perennials, all constrained with well-clipped
edges and hedges. In autumn the colours of the shimmering European
aspen (*Populus tremula*), established copper beech and birch planted by
an earlier garden owner, tulip trees and ornamental grapes produce a rich
range of yellows, russets and reds. In winter, the garden's strong design
becomes even more evident.

The 1.5-hectare garden was laid out during the late 1990s to create a park-
like landscape of uncluttered spaces that afford views to the surrounding

Opposite: Dawn lights the parterre at Jack's Ridge: hedges of well-clipped box
constrain plantings of *Lavandula angustifolia* and *Hebe* 'Inspiration'. An avenue
of Manchurian pear (*Pyrus ussuriensis*) leads to the parterre, parallel with a series
of arbours covered in Boston ivy, *Parthenocissus tricuspidata*.

hills and distant Port Phillip Bay. Strong bones are provided by clipped hedges, avenues of carefully chosen and perfectly maintained trees, and walls of local stone.

This garden comprises beautiful rooms of squares and rectangles. An avenue of Manchurian pears, with a bronze fountain providing a central focal point, forms one of several axes: this one is aligned with an arch smothered in the pink and white rose 'Pierre de Ronsard'. Anchored by a pair of clipped ligustrum obelisks, the arch leads through a long border of the white Hybrid Tea rose 'Seduction' into a walled vegetable garden.

This soft and pretty garden, replete with blooming roses, detailed perennial borders and burgeoning vegetable beds, thrives in a tough gardening country: Australia is a land of regular and ruthless drought. Not a drop of rainwater is wasted, as the Jacks are totally reliant on the rain—they have no springs. Every drop that falls is cleverly caught: bluestone

Opposite, top: This clever parterre of lavender, box and hebe at Jack's Ridge camouflages a 100 000-litre underground water-tank. The lavender is clipped into tight balls each year after flowering, to prevent it from becoming 'leggy'. *Opposite, bottom left to right:* An arch of *Rosa* 'Pierre de Ronsard'; the Manchurian pear walk; a shaded spot on the front lawn. *Above:* Thirty-centimetre thick ironbark posts for the grapevine-covered arbour were salvaged from a bridge. The penstemon 'Evelyn', pink with a white throat, white foxgloves and the white rose 'Sally Holmes' bloom in the gardens that skirt the pergola.

Above: Walls throughout the garden at Jack's Ridge are of a soft-coloured local stone, hand-selected from the quarry to ensure there were no strong oranges. Steps lead to the croquet lawn surrounded by a hedge of myrtle, *Luma apiculata.* **Opposite:** A border of the white Hybrid Tea rose 'Seduction' runs along the wall that protects the vegetable garden, which is accessed by an arch smothered in the pink and white *R.* 'Pierre de Ronsard'—a French-bred rose named after the poet, who died in 1585 and is buried at La Riche, Brittany.

guttering on paths and driveways, and a system of underground drains, direct all rainwater into a dam. Rainwater from the house roof supplies the 100 000-litre underground domestic water-tank.

Susan and Graeme also attribute the success of the garden to the regular application of a rich mulch mixed with poultry manure, which produces spectacular results. They also acknowledge that the garden was well prepared at the outset. Truckloads of soil were brought in for the lawn areas, and they are blessed with rich, red, slightly acidic soil. Susan's observation that 'things grow' is an understatement.

WATER DELIGHTS

Water: mystical, mythical, musical and mesmerising. It is the lifeblood of civilisations and can dictate the ethos of a people. It can break a nation's heart, and bestow great riches. The Persians understood it, and it has demanded a central place in all garden cultures since before the time of Christ.

Garden writers, designers and owners have always understood the importance of water in the garden.

Holker Hall

To see a World in a Grain of Sand
And a Heaven in a Wild Flower,
Hold infinity in the palm of your hand
And Eternity in an hour.

WILLIAM BLAKE, 'AUGURIES OF INNOCENCE', VERSE 1

If the thought of standing twenty deep in the display tent at those famous English Horticultural Shows, then moving at a snail's pace as part of one massive, amorphous body of people, does not appeal, the Holker Garden Festival, sited in the 10 hectares of gardens that surround one of England's loveliest private houses, could be for you.

Holker Hall gardens, created within the gentle maritime climate of Morecambe Bay and under the kindly influences of the Gulf Stream, are reached via the coastal village of Grange-Over-Sands, at the very southern end of England's Lake District. If you eschew the garden shop—often difficult, as the English do the farm shops that accompany historic houses and gardens so well—you immediately enter a lesson in garden history. This is by no means simply a tourist garden, however: these gardens have been created through centuries of private ownership by keen plantsmen and -women. For those interested in stately houses and their furnishings, the 'hall' of priceless family treasures provides its own lesson in the decorative and fine arts.

Home to Lord and Lady Cavendish, the present Holker Hall dates from 1871, after much of an earlier Elizabethan house was destroyed by fire.

Opposite: Holker Hall, located on the southern tip of England's Lake District, is photographed in May, from the Summer Garden. On the site of a former tennis court, the Summer Garden is backed by tall hedges of beech, which afford protection to deep borders of spring bulbs.

Above: An *allée* of perfectly clipped Portuguese laurel dissects the summer garden at Holker Hall and leads towards the parkland and meadows. *Opposite, top:* In the Elliptical Garden, arches are covered in the old self-pollinating variety of flowering apple, *Malus* 'Lord Lambourne'. *Opposite, bottom:* In the Summer Garden, perimeter beds are filled with spring bulbs and edged with box. English gardens make great use of annual prunings of hazelnuts, willow and fruit trees to create plant supports—wigwams, square and rectangular cages, and domes—to prevent tall-growing perennials such as delphiniums and foxgloves from collapsing over other plants.

The original Holker Hall, steeped in generations of English history, goes back to the Dissolution of the Monasteries, which began in 1536.

The house is set on wide terraces, created with slate from the estate's quarries, which give way immediately to the large elliptical and rectangular summer gardens. In the borders of these formal gardens, intricate plantings of perennials feature delphiniums supported by cages and tripods woven each year from coppiced hazelnuts. Yew and box hedges add further structure. Screens and arbours of pleached laurel, lime and apple extend from the house to lead the visitor through these formal gardens and out to the wildflower meadows and collections of rare and important trees.

The gardens were first laid out formally in the early eighteenth century. A parkland of wonderful trees was added later that century, with the arrival of the fashion for creating natural-looking landscape gardens. In the nineteenth century, advice was sought from the legendary Sir Joseph Paxton (1801–1865), gardener to the 6th Duke of Devonshire at the massive Chatsworth gardens in Derbyshire. In the tradition of many of the great gardens,

WATER DELIGHTS

plants were obtained from the plant hunters, whose great expeditions were sponsored by the leading families: a large monkey puzzle tree, for instance, was grown from seed brought from Chile by William Lobb in 1844.

In the higher reaches of the gardens, the rose garden, created in the early twentieth century by the British designer Thomas Mawson (1861–1933), is best accessed through the wildflower meadow via a massive curved pergola covered with wisteria and honeysuckle.

Central to the gardens at Holker Hall is the extraordinary Neptune Cascade, which tumbles down either edge of a steep staircase that almost dissects the lower section of the grounds. Fed by a series of underground streams, it descends from a terrace towards the top of the gardens under a forest of mature rhododendrons and delicate tree ferns, past swaths of hostas, to finish at the base of the garden in an elliptical pool. There, a water spout ensures movement and musicality. There is both beauty and excitement at every turn.

Opposite, top: The lovely rose garden at Holker Hall was designed during Lady Moyra Cavendish's tenure from 1908 to 1946.
Opposite, bottom left to right: Elegant twin pavilions connect each end of the half-moon-shaped rose garden; the wild garden; a delicate arbour in the rose garden curtained with heavily scented honeysuckle. *Above:* The Neptune Cascade travels down twin stone staircases to a pool and fountain, edged with tree ferns (*Dicksonia antarctica*) and hostas. These flourish under a pink-to-red flowering *Rhododendron arboreum*, introduced from the Himalayas in 1810 and the parent of many hybrids.

Le Canadel

How should the man of taste, who seeks only simple and genuine pleasures, plan a walk at the very door of his house? He must make it so convenient and agreeable that he can enjoy it at every hour of the day.

SWISS PHILOSOPHER AND LITERARY FIGURE JEAN-JACQUES ROUSSEAU (1712–1778)

In the Var region of southern France, among the hills behind St Tropez, a large garden has been developed over several decades by an Australian couple. At its centre is a 2-hectare lake, fed by the multitude of springs that emanate from the highest part of the property, and from the mountains beyond. Water—or *la source*, as the French somewhat mysteriously call it—was one of the elements among a set of four essentials submitted to land agents by the couple, who have long called this part of France home.

An agricultural area, the Var is washed with the blues of lavenders and rosemaries, greys of olive trees and greens of pines. The patterns of the soil are drawn in trellised grapevines and reflected in roofs ribbed with rounded, soft terracotta tiles.

The house and its surrounding farmland were bought in 1993 after an extensive search. It fulfilled all the requirements: as well as having plentiful running water, the property is within 90 minutes of Monaco, where the owners live for much of the year. It has the ancient plane trees that contribute to the vernacular of the region, and the house is a *bastide* or important country house, with long windows and high ceilings, rather than the simple farmhouse known as a *mas* (pronounced 'mar').

Opposite: Two mature horse chestnuts (*Aesculus hippocastanum*) and a massive bull bay magnolia (*Magnolia grandiflora*) shade the lawn that stretches out from the house at Le Canadel. The house, once the centre of a large farm, retains its original pink wash and is cooled by blue-painted shutters.

Built in two parts between 1750 and 1780, this country house was once the focus of an important farm in the area, producing grapes, wheat and other crops. Since its inception, the property has been known as Le Canadel which, in the local Provençal patois, means a canal of water.

Today the garden unfolds from a mellow, pink-washed house, its elegant façade and windows enhanced by blue-painted shutters with a terracotta rim—originally, each shutter was a different colour.

About 15 hectares of wine grapes and olives thrive in the hot summers of the region. The local white grape *Vitis* 'Rolle' (in Italy it is called 'Vermentino' and is popular with growers in other tough climates) is made into a fresh, slightly spicy, crisp wine by the local oenologist. As well as the *Olea* 'Aglandau' variety of olives, in deference to a system of appellation that is soon to be introduced for the olive industry, the local cultivar 'Cayon' is grown.

Opposite, top: A long iron arbour, covered in wisteria, *Rosa* 'New Dawn' and Chinese star jasmine provides a canopy over the terrace that skirts the house at Le Canadel. *Opposite, bottom left*: Fondly known as La Porcherie—as it once housed the farm's pigs—this garden shed supports 'Wedding Day' and 'Ballerina' roses. *Opposite, bottom centre*: *Rosa* 'Dr Huey' blooms a clear red on the oldest part of the house. *Opposite, bottom right*: An ancient, rustic iron gate leads into the rose parterre. *Above*: This lovely garden room was once a garage with an earthen floor.

Above, left: Plane trees and the traditional, and tough, white mulberry tree shade the boule court. The court was built along the property's eastern boundary to provide a break for the summer bushfires, which can suddenly whip up, assisted by the ferocious mistral winds.
Above, centre: Just one species of lavender, *Lavandula angustifolia*—which copes with the very cold winters—is grown on the lavender court. A terracotta artichoke, purchased in a Sydney antique shop many years ago, is centre stage. **Above, right:** A heavily scented *Philadelphus* grows alongside a beautiful old stone trough, near the main entrance to the house.
Opposite: A traditional stone fountain in front of the house is shaded by mature plane trees.

The Tuscan olive 'Frantoia', with its decorative, spreading branches, is also grown; not only is it a prettier tree, but it is well suited to the very cold winters and hot summers of the area, similar to those of Tuscany.

Over many years of gardening in different climates around the world, the owners have learned to work in harmony with their environment. In the Var they grow species that thrive in its climate and alkaline soil, although, wherever they garden, several much-loved plants are always on their list, among them white 'Iceberg' roses—easygoing and generous. The shell-pink climber 'New Dawn' is also a favourite: its blush-pink tones blend perfectly with the grey-greens of much of the foliage in the garden. Chinese star jasmine (*Trachelospermum jasminoides*) is used repeatedly to wonderful, scented effect, as is wisteria, which covers the iron pergola that runs the length of the eastern half of the house, feeding out from the dark, shady garden room. Other white plants considered 'must-haves' include Japanese anemones, the heavily scented philadelphus, and choisya, which does so well that it has been used as hedges throughout the garden. Ginkgos, only recently introduced to the West from their native China, are always planted.

Irises—many in the darkest of blues and gifted from the nearby garden La Casella (*see* pages 225–9)—thrive in the tough conditions: winter temperatures drop to -15 degrees Celcius at night and summer days can reach 40 degrees Celcius, with rain-free periods of up to ten weeks. And the owner revels in the scents of rosemary and thyme when she walks through the local bushland of pine and oak. She loves pruning, hedging and dead-heading the roses.

Although on a grand scale, this lovely farm garden appears—perhaps somewhat deceptively—completely natural, and is perfectly at home in its setting. The colours that hover in the summer haze—the blues and lavenders, the pinks and occasional apricot and, most importantly, white—leave you with a vivid sense of place.

Mona

Brown's forte was the middle distance landscape garden: scenes of sweeping turf accentuated by groups of noble trees casting long shadows, contours sloping to glimpses of a broad winding river and rising beyond to melt into the skyline of encircling woodlands.

CHRISTOPHER HUSSEY IN DOROTHY STROUD, *CAPABILITY BROWN*, **P. 33**

It is difficult to believe that Kerry and Greg Schneider have not yet made the pilgrimage to the great landscaped gardens of the United Kingdom, but have simply visited them during their extensive reading on the best landscapes in the world.

When the Schneiders bought Mona at Braidwood in the Southern Tablelands of New South Wales in the mid 1990s, they inherited a well-known and much-loved 5-hectare garden of mature, cold-climate trees, sweeping lawns and an enchanting walled garden. Since arriving, the Schneiders have built upon this horticultural heritage and extended the garden, influenced by their research into the eighteenth-century English landscape masters.

Braidwood, the first entire town to be listed on the State Heritage Register (including for the preservation of rural vistas from the township),

Opposite, left: The house at Mona—built of stone in 1901 after the original 1830s homestead was destroyed by fire—is shaded by mature, northern hemisphere trees, and looks over terraced gardens. *Left*: The bronze sculpture 'Torso' is by artist Patricia Lawrence; it stands in a circle of mophead robinias.

has been at the centre of the region's pastoral industry since first settled by Scottish immigrants early in the nineteenth century. An important wool-growing region, this is tough gardening country, however, with winters that can reach –10 degrees Celcius and summers that can be hot and dry; soils are largely granitic.

To protect the property from the ravages of the elements, including icy winds that hit suddenly from July to September, the Schneiders have planted more than 4000 trees throughout the garden and in its surrounding paddocks. Dozens of beech accompany 800 small-leaved linden (*Tilia cordata*) and 500 plane trees, along with horse chestnuts and generous copses of red oak (*Quercus rubra*). Stands of holly oak (*Quercus ilex*) which, although evergreen, can survive the ruthless frosts this district experiences, further protect the garden. A double avenue of pin oaks (*Quercus palustris*), which colours a dramatic crimson each April, has been planted along one boundary of the property.

Linking the original formal gardens—laid out on several levels around the stone homestead—with the maturing parkland and surrounding rural views is an expansive, half-hectare lake, built a decade ago. Edged with water-purifying grasses—including the vigorous, bamboo-like common reed (*Phragmites australis*) with its autumn plumes, and the club rush (*Schoenoplectus validus*)—it is now home to platypus and black swans. Swaths of

Opposite, top: Deep borders of the orange double daylily (*Hemerocallis fulva* 'Kwanso') tone with the mellow stone that dresses Mona's buildings. *Opposite, bottom*: Hedges of *Viburnum farreri* define the boundary between the upper and lower lawns. The beautiful finials that top an old, curved wall mark where stage coaches once arrived. *Top, left*: The historic 1903 coach house has been converted into luxurious accommodation. *Top, centre*: Dwarf white agapanthus (*Agapanthus* 'Snowball') and *Sedum* 'Autumn Joy' add constant interest to the garden bed that hugs the tennis pavilion. Tubs of *Thuja orientalis* stand guard around the pavilion. *Top, right*: A quiet seat beckons on the stone-flagged verandah. *Above*: Three sixty-year-old broad-leaved lindens (*Tilia platyphyllos*) provide shade on the upper lawn.

Above: Beyond Mona's original walled garden, and on the western side of the house, a lead urn rests within a parterre of quarters, formed from doubled hedges of clipped *Lonicera nitida* and box, each segment filled with spring bulbs. A dense green backdrop is created by a dozen western red cedar (*Thuja plicata*), just a decade old, but looking as if they have been there forever. *Opposite, top*: The original stage coach road that led into the property during the nineteenth century. *Opposite, bottom*: The five-arch stone bridge was commissioned by the owners in 1999 and constructed by local builders. It was inspired by the work of the sixteenth-century architect Andrea Palladio.

river oaks (*Casuarina cunninghamiana*) act as a windbreak against the north-westerly winds, which were causing erosion of the lake banks and battering the blooms in the formal rose garden.

After careful tree surgery, the dark and mysterious elm woods have been opened up to create lines of sight through the garden spaces. The pathways that wind through this woodland are bordered with jonquils and daffodils, which bloom from midwinter; this display is followed by a carpet of bluebells in late September and hundreds of spectacular rhododendrons in mid to late spring.

Kerry Schneider's favourite plant in the garden is *Viburnum × burkwoodii*, because the autumn leaves glow a soft ruby-red, and in spring it produces clusters of heavenly scented white flowers.

After years of care, the orchard's ancient cherry, plum and pear trees are again laden with fruit, adding to a regular autumn bounty of apples and quinces. And there is much, much more in this awe-inspiring yet restful garden.

PLACES TO PRAY IN

Simplicity is a characteristic central to many great gardens, and one that is sure to impart a sense of calm. And it is a quality that makes Japanese gardens among the most peaceful in the world. Respectful of centuries of cultural, religious and literary history, Japanese gardens employ great discipline and restraint.

The spiritual meets the intellectual in these gardens, and demands that one slows down and rests; contemplates and prays.

Ninna-ji

The sapling cherry Genji had planted the year before sent out a scattering of blossoms, the air was soft and warm, and memories flooded back, bringing him often to tears.

MURASAKI SHIKIBU, *THE TALE OF GENJI*, THE GREAT
LITERARY WORK OF THE HEIAN PERIOD (781–1185)

Coupled with an appreciation of the notions of restraint and understatement, an intense connection with nature is central to the Japanese aesthetic and is demonstrated in all aspects of its culture, from painting and literature to cuisine and garden-making.

Part of that engagement with nature is a reverence for the changing seasons, acknowledged in many ways, from the sweets made by specialist shops in Kyoto's ancient Gion quarter, to the markings on a tea bowl, or street and shop decorations. And nowhere is this sensitivity more clearly demonstrated than during the few brief days of cherry blossom.

During *hanami*, or cherry blossom viewing, the Japanese—many of whom are dressed in kimonos that honour the season—flock to sites such as Kyoto's Nijo Castle and Kiyomizu Temple, where hundreds of trees in full bloom are floodlit at night.

Horticultural purists love single blooms—species roses, single peonies and delicate, wild lilac—but to see avenues of single, five-petalled, blush-pink cherry blossom, held on contorted soot-black branches, is to be

Opposite: In the eastern compound at Ninna-ji, the five-storey pagoda, the Kondo—moved from the Imperial Palace in 1630 during the Edo Period reconstruction of the complex—rises above a copse of 'Omuro' cherry blossom in early April.

converted to restraint. The *sakura* or Japanese flowering cherries, which line the streets throughout Japan, are chosen from several different species and varieties, most of them hybrids of *Prunus speciosa* and *P. serrulata*; many have been under cultivation for more than a thousand years.

Nowhere is the sense of nature as a muse more intense than at Kyoto's ancient imperial temple, Ninna-ji, which nestles into the base of the low mountains to the west of the city. It is only there that you will find the 'Omuro' variety of cherry, which bears a larger and paler—although still single—flower.

Completed in 888 as a large complex of more than 60 sub-temples, Ninna-ji was destroyed during the Onin Wars of 1467–1477. It was rebuilt on a more modest scale by the Tokugawa shogunate in the seventeenth century—during the Edo Period (1600–1868)—and is now World Heritage listed. With its beautiful rustic buildings, exquisite painted screens and important entrance gate, Ninna-ji holds a special significance for many Japanese. It was the first temple to become a *monzeki*, a temple with a head priest—an abbot—provided by the imperial family, a tradition that continued from 888 to 1869.

Divided into three compounds, the main gardens at Ninna-ji are located in the south-eastern section. There, the gardens are designed on two levels and divided into north and south gardens. The north garden—of raked gravel, ponds and pine-covered hillside, where a delicate teahouse is perched—is designed to be viewed from the main building, with its severe angles. It is a perfect example of a balanced compositon: the foreground, the middle

Opposite, top: The ideal of rustic beauty—*kirei sabi*—is embodied in the thatched imperial entrance gate to Ninna-ji's south-eastern compound. **Opposite, bottom:** The garden is framed by the austere angles of the temple buildings. Here, a rustic outdoor corridor links the main building, the Shinden, to an outbuilding in the north garden, so that the garden may be viewed from different angles—demonstrating the Chinese influence on Japanese architecture during the Heian Period. **Above:** The north garden, dating from the fourteenth century, includes several small ponds, a single-stone bridge and great expanses of raked gravel. In Japanese gardens, a selection of rakes is used: gravel might be arranged each morning with a different rake to reflect the weather and change of seasons. A swirling pattern might reflect expected wind or a raindrop pattern of ripples moving out from a central point, pending inclement weather.

Above: At another Kyoto temple, Tenryu-ji, an example of borrowed views. *Opposite:* *Sakura*, or cherry blossom, is the unofficial national flower of Japan. In Kyoto, canals, rivers and roads are lined with *sakura* and clouds of pale blossom foreground austere wooden temples; hillsides are peppered with wild cherry trees that have also invaded the bamboo forests covering the mountains that almost ring the city.

ground of pond and a narrow path leading across a stone bridge, and the background of planted hillside. The more simple south garden is dominated by a spreading pine, its heavy, sweeping horizontal branches reverently supported by wooden crutches.

Ninna-ji features in Japanese literature, most notably as the setting for much of *The Tale of Genji*, written around 1000AD by Lady Murasaki, a noblewoman of the imperial court. Along with much of Japanese literature, this six-volume saga describes the aesthetic preoccupations of the nobility of the period, and illustrates an acute awareness of the transitory nature of life, of human frailty and of the imperfection of beauty. The fleeting presence of the cherry blossom is one example of this daily sensibility.

Saiho-ji

After the garden
Had been swept clean,
Some camellia flowers fell down.

YAHA, 'SPRING'

There are more than one hundred and twenty species of moss in the gardens at Saiho-ji temple, known to English speakers as the Moss Garden. Possibly the world's most serene landscape, this 2-hectare, cathedral-like garden has been listed as a UNESCO World Heritage site since 1994.

Owned by members of the Rinzai Zen Buddhist sect, the garden is nestled in the foothills of the mountains on the north-western edge of the ancient capital of Kyoto and incorporates several different moods.

In 1339, a leading Zen priest and gifted landscape gardener, Muso Soseki (1275–1351), set about reconstructing a garden first built on the site in the Nara Period (710–794); the garden had been severely damaged during Japan's fierce civil wars.

Even though very different in atmosphere from other dry-garden landscapes, Saiho-ji is thought to be Japan's first *kare sansui* garden, considered the precursor to all dry gardens in the country, including the more famous rock garden at Ryo¯an-ji (*see* pages 155–9). It is also said that the Ashikaga shoguns—Yoshimitsu and Yoshimasa—were inspired by the

Opposite: Located throughout Saiho-ji's serene grounds are more than 120 species of moss flowing over the ground in a soft, cool blanket of green. Even the bridges, linking the small islands throughout the ponds, have not escaped the soothing verdant wave.

rock formations in this garden and by the Muso sensibilities, when they constructed the less discreet gold pavilion (Kinkaku-ji) and silver pavilion, Ginkaku-ji.

The Saiho-ji garden—which is today probably very different from that designed in the fourteenth century—is best appreciated in three parts. The entrance point is a void, an expanse of white gravel, which is dominated in April by a massive flowering cherry, its bloom-laden branches sweeping the ground. Nearby is the beautiful, austere wooden temple hall, where the visitor is asked to take part in a short ceremony in preparation for the contemplative nature of the garden. A mantra is chanted by the priests, while the seated visitor copies an ancient text with a thick calligraphy brush; the process is intended to clear and purify the mind before walking through the dark gates into another world.

Opposite, top: Saiho-ji's priests wish to keep its solemn, peaceful atmosphere intact: visitors are asked to take part in a ceremony to prepare for quiet contemplation in the garden. *Opposite, bottom left:* The entrance to the lower pond garden is reached via a curving path of stepping stones. *Opposite, bottom centre:* The islands within the pond represent the Buddhist notion of paradise. *Opposite, bottom right:* This rustic hut enhances the appreciation of pastoral simplicity and connection to nature. *Above:* In early April the monochromatic tones of the entrance court-yard are lit by a flowering cherry.

Above: At Saiho-ji, set in the cool shadow of the mountain, spring comes a little later. Here the purple azalea is about to bloom. *Opposite:* Saiho-ji was not planned as a moss garden—the moss appeared naturally in the low light and adds to its mystique and allure.

The most extraordinary part of this garden is undoubtedly its vast collection of different moss species, in a variety of textures and greens—from glistening emerald to brilliant, bright yellow-green, all of which have grown here naturally. In the lower garden, which wraps around a meandering stream, light reflects upon the still water and velvety moss, which has spread out naturally in undulating contours in the dappled shadows of the forest of black-stemmed pines. In this supremely restful atmosphere only the occasional fallen crimson bloom of a camellia interrupts the mood of contemplation and simplicity.

The upper garden climbs through a bamboo forest to a low hill, and further, past a dry waterfall. Here tranquil, flat-topped rocks appear more sympathetic to the horizontal lines of the landscape in this country of islands, in contrast with the vertical rocks (which have taken their inspiration from the gardens of the Chinese Song Period, 960–1279) at nearby Tenryu-ji.

The random sound of the bamboo deer scarer is all that breaks the silence in the garden, which encapsulates perfectly the ideals of *sabi*—the patina of age—and *wabi*—naturalness, simplicity, imperfection.

And I have heard that Saiho-ji is at its best just after rain: that I want to experience.

PLACES TO PLAY IN

Golf is something of a mystery to those who don't indulge—but not, however, to the millions of sportspeople of varying ability who understand it. For those who love the game, the chance to walk in sublime settings, in good company and fresh air, all in the name of exercise, is intoxicating. Some golf courses have been laid out against a backdrop of soaring mountains, others along coastlines, emulating the scenes in which Scottish shepherds foreshadowed the game by hitting rocks across fields with their crooks. That they are often set, today, among glorious gardens is an added bonus.

Golf Courses

OF

Kauai

Golf is more than a game ... It is played in the mountains, the desert, the jungle, the rain forest and inside volcanic craters. It is played on cliffs, prairies, islands and farmland. It has even been played on the moon.

EDITORS OF *THE GOLF INSIDER, GOLF TRAVEL BY DESIGN*, P. XI

For some people, the idea of paradise is a golf course. Not only is there the physical and intellectual challenge of outsmarting the layout, but also the joy of playing the game in, most often, wonderful settings. Even if you don't have a passion for golf, the island of Kauai—home to several of the world's greatest golf courses—might appear an Eden. Justly dubbed 'The Garden Isle', Kauai is a 1430-square-kilometre jewel of rich volcanic soil and high rainfall in which tropical plants—both native and exotic—flourish. The island was discovered by Polynesian voyagers some 2000 years ago: its towering, jungle-covered mountains melt into the clear sea, and groves of palms bend and sway over dozens of white, sandy beaches. Several of the island's courses boast holes with iconic reputations, talked about by golfers around the world: set in Kauai's mesmerising natural landscape, they are beautiful enough to distract any player from their stroke.

Many of the golf courses come replete with their own magnificent gardens. Among the three courses designed in Kauai by golf architect Robert Trent Jones Jnr (b. 1939), the 180-hectare Poipu Bay Golf Course, on the

Opposite: The extraordinary landscape on Kauai provides a canvas for a wealth of species, earning it the title of 'The Garden Isle'. Here, Limahuli Botanic Gardens, a repository for many endangered Hawaiian species, is located on the island's north shore and is surrounded by towering peaks.

south-eastern side of the island, provides a stage for performances by many of Hawaii's most flamboyant indigenous plants.

Landscaped with hibiscus species, which contribute so much to the aesthetic of Hawaiian gardens, the highly scented evergreen frangipani (*Plumeria obtusa*), and coconut palms (*Cocus nucifera*), which bow in response to decades of gentle off-shore breezes, this course is backed by emerald-green mountains and sculpted from a volcanic plateau, some eight storeys above the Pacific Ocean.

Close by is the Allerton Garden, the site of the former retreat of the Hawaiian Queen Emma who, two centuries ago, had great quantities of exotic species transported there. Today one of several properties owned by the National Tropical Botanical Garden, the 4.5-hectare garden was established by the amateur botanist and plant hunter Robert Allerton after he purchased the estate in 1938. At that time, it was neglected and overrun by succulents, remnants of which remain: agaves, aloes, cotyledons, crassulas, and the indestructible mother-in-law's tongue, *Sansevieria trifasciata*. This plant has recently become popular again, though it can become weedy and is difficult to eradicate in tropical climates: on Kauai it has escaped from an early European settler's garden. It copes well with shade but, if given sunshine, flowers with scented cream spikes at night.

Opposite, top: The glorious countryside at the north end of Kauai is best seen from Hanalei Lookout. *Opposite, bottom*: Ground covers of oyster plant (*Tradescantia spathacea*) can withstand salt-laden breezes on the Prince Course, Princeville. *Top*: In the south of the island, mass plantings of *Hibiscus rosa-sinensis* ensure a holiday atmosphere at the Poipu Course. *Above, left to right*: Hibiscus hybrid; *H. mutabilis*; *H. rosa-sinensis*; *Plumeria* 'Carmen'; the torch ginger (*Etlingera elatior*); *Codiaeum variegatum*.

Although these gardens have suffered the onslaught of several recent cyclones, they remain a lush, tropical paradise overlaid on a classical design, all in a hidden valley that runs inland from the picturesque and romantic Lawai-Kai Cove.

On the wetter north shore of the island are two famous golf courses, laid out along a rugged coastline and in the shadow of glowering mountains, dominated by the twin peaks of Hihimanu. At Princeville Resort, two courses designed by Robert Trent Jones Jnr are set in an extraordinary landscape: they overlook Hanalei Bay and the beach where the movie *South Pacific* was filmed in 1958. From the Championship tees, there are spectacular 360-degree views across Kauai's dramatic north shore.

These courses showcase the tropical plants of the island, most particularly the fascinating and fragrant frangipanis for which it is noted. But they are also golf courses for those who love danger and employ Jones's 'risk and reward' strategy. Some of the holes are famous, spoken of by devotees with a mix of bravura and awe.

On the Prince Course—named after Prince Albert, the only son of King Kamehameha IV and Queen Emma and considered the best in Hawaii—the designer's favourite is the challenging fifteenth hole: 527 metres with the tee shot across a jungle-filled ravine. Fun for long hitters, but a trap for golf balls. Accuracy onto the green is also essential: ravines snarl on either side and a front sand trap deters you from settling for a running shot.

Other holes to excite passionate golfers are the seventh—a par 3 hole at 187 metres and overlooking beautiful Anini Beach—and the thirteenth—a demanding par 4 boasting a natural waterfall behind the green.

There are memorable holes, too, on the adjacent Makai course, with its impressive carpets of tradescantia, drapery of bamboo and stands of tall palms. The course is made up of three spectacular nine-hole courses: Ocean Nine, Lakes Nine and Woods Nine. The seventh hole on Ocean Nine is billed as one of the world's best golf holes, demanding a tee shot over the Pacific Ocean, with the 'Queens Bath' far below, cut by crashing waves into the coastal cliffs. The fifth on the Lakes runs along the ocean and is a drivable par 4.

Nearby and just past Hanalei Bay and Tunnels Beach—an iconic spot for surfers—the world's largest collection of rare and endangered tropical plants thrives in Limahuli Garden and Preserve. After restoration of the site's ecosystem, there are native fan palms, bell flowers, rare hibiscus, taro (*Colocasia esculenta*) and other indigenous food plants. A new US$21 million Botanical Research Centre was completed there in January 2008.

It is particularly poignant, then, to learn that Hawaii has more plants facing extinction than any other region in the world—but Kauai does, indeed, continue to enjoy the feel of an unspoiled tropical paradise. And for golfers who constantly set themselves personal goals—a full round beating their par, perhaps, or a lower handicap—one must be to play the Kauai courses. This is my kind of Eden.

GARDEN CONTACT
DETAILS AND ADDRESSES

Gardens are listed below as they appear in the book. If a garden does not appear, it is because it is not open to the public or, as with the gardens in Iran, are best visited using a local tour guide. Gardens belonging to a hotel are open to dining and hotel guests only.

   Opening times can also vary from year to year; where they are not given below, please check the website. Contact details and opening times were correct at the time of publication, but it is important to check them before visiting, by phone, email or online.

VILLA LANTE

Bagnaia, 1 hour north of Rome, Italy
Open All year, except Mon and public hols.
9 am–6.30 pm (4 pm in winter). Combine with nearby Palazzo Farnese (guided tour booking essential: Tourism Italia at www.enit.it).

HAREWOOD HOUSE

Harewood, Leeds LS17 9LQ, England
Open All year, but weekends only in Nov, Dec, Feb and early Mar, 10 am–6 pm
C + 44 (0) 113 218 1010
@ business@harewood.org
W www.harewood.org

GRAVETYE MANOR

Near East Grinstead, West Sussex RH19 4LJ, England
Open Garden open to dining and hotel guests only
C + 44 (0) 134 281 0567
FAX + 44 (0) 134 281 0080
W www.gravetyemanor.co.uk

THE MANOR HOUSE

Upton Grey, Hampshire RG25 2RD, England
Open Garden by appointment on weekdays
@ uptongrey.garden@lineone.net

HESTERCOMBE

Cheddon Fitzpaine, Taunton, Somerset TA2 8LG, England
Open Daily (except Christmas Day) 10 am–6 pm
C + 44 (0) 18 2341 3923
FAX + 44 (0) 18 2341 3747
@ info@hestercombe.com
W www.hestercombegardens.com

ZHUOZHENG YUAN

No. 178 Dongbei Street, Suzhou, China
Open 7.30 am–5.30 pm
C 86 512 6751 0286
W www.suzhou.gov.cn/English/Travel

NINFA

Cisterna, near the village of Sermonetta, Italy
Open Limited times (guided tours only).
Write to Ninfa, Fondazione Caetani, Via Ninfina, Doganella di Ninfa, Cisterna, Latina
C + 39 (0) 6687 3056

LES JARDINS DU PARADIS

Place du Théron, 81170 Cordes-sur-Ciel, France
Open Daily end April – beginning Oct
C + 33 (0) 5 6356 2977
@ cordes.development@wanadoo.fr

COTTESBROOKE HALL

Northampton, NN6 8PF, England
Open Tues–Fri Easter–Sept,
also weekends in Sept, 2–5 pm
C + 44 (0) 16 0450 5808
FAX + 44 (0) 16 0450 5619
@ enquiries@cottesbrooke.co.uk
W www.cottesbrookehall.co.uk

THUYA GARDEN
(AND ASTICOU TERRACES PRESERVE)

Seal Harbor Rd (Rte 3), Northeast Harbor, Maine, USA
Open Daily late June – Sept, 7 am–7 pm
C (summer) + 1 207 276 5130
C (winter) +1 207 276 3727
W www.visitmaine.com
Park at Thuya Lodge or walk up the cliff trail

BENTLEY

Close to Bentley, in Tasmania's Chudleigh Valley, is historic Old WesleyDale, also part of Native Plain, and the Travers Hartley Vaughan 1829 land grant. To visit, or stay, at Old WesleyDale:
C 61 (0)3 6363 1212
@ tassiedevil76@hotmail.comor
W www.oldwesleydaleheritage.com

THE DESIGNER IN THE GARDEN

VILLA VALMARANA AI NANI
Via dei Nani 8, 36100 Vicenza, Italy
Open Mar–Nov, Tues–Sun 10 am–12 pm,
Wed, Thur, Sat and Sun 3–6 pm
C FAX + 39 432 1803
@ valmarana@villavalmarana.com
W www.villavalmarana.com
For guided walks of Palladian sites, dinners held
in the villas, and concerts and operas in Teatro
Olimpico, contact Vicenza Tourism: www.vicenzae
.org or email info@vicenzae.org

NAUMKEAG
Prospect Hill Rd, Stockbridge, Massachusetts, USA
Open Memorial Day (30 May) – Columbus Day
(12 Oct), 10 am–5 pm
C + 1 413 298 8146
@ westregion@ttor.org
Close by is Tanglewood, summer home of the
Boston Symphony (see www.bso.org)

The Emerald Necklace Conservancy
W www.emeraldnecklace.org

Isabella Stewart Gardner Museum, Boston
W www.gardnermuseum.org

The Mount
Puenkett St, Lenox, Massachusetts, USA
Open Daily, May–Oct, 9 am–5 pm
C + 1 413 637 1899
W www.edithwharton.org

STEVENS-COOLIDGE PLACE
Andover St, North Andover, Massachusetts, USA
Open Guided tours of house: end May – mid Oct,
Sat–Sun 1–4 pm; of garden: by appointment for
groups of 10 or more
@ neregion@ttor.org
W www.spnea.org or www.thetrustees.org/
pages/366_stevens_coolidge_place.cfm

DUMBARTON OAKS
R and 31st Sts, NW, Washington DC, USA
Open Gardens daily (except national holidays)
April–Oct 2–6 pm; Nov–Mar 2–5 pm
C +1 202 342 3212 for opening times of the rare
book library and collections rooms
W www.doaks.org

NEW SUZHOU MUSEUM GARDEN
No. 204 Dongbei Street, Suzhou, China
Open 9.00 am–5.00 pm
C 86 512 6757 5666
FAX 86 512 6754 4232
@ admin@szmuseum.com
W www.szmuseum.com/szbwgen

KYOTO'S ANCIENT GARDENS
Buses go directly to all gardens from Kyoto
Central Station.

For Imperial Gardens in Kyoto, www.kunaicho.go
.jp/eindex.html or, on your first day in Kyoto, visit
the Imperial Household Office with your passport
and ask to join a group.

Shiro Nakane Landscaping
@ nakane@lares.dti.ne.jp
W www.nakane-garden.co.jp

POLITICIANS' GARDENS

JICHANG YUAN
Xihui Park, Huishan bystreet, Wuxi, China
Open 8.00 am–5.30 pm
C 86 510 8370 8324

MOUNT VERNON ESTATE
3200 Mt Vernon Memorial Hwy, Mt Vernon,
Virginia, USA
Open Daily all year 9 am–4 pm
C 703 780 2000
@ info@mtvernon.org
W www.mountvernon.org

MONTICELLO
931 Thomas Jefferson Parkway, Charlottesville,
Virginia, USA
Open Daily except Christmas: Mar–Oct 8 am–5 pm;
Nov–Feb 9 am–4.30
C 434 984 9822
W www.monticello.org
Virginia Garden Week, held each April, opens
hundreds of private homes and gardens: email
gdnweek@erols.com, or www.vagardenweek.org
or www.virginia.org

WRITERS' GARDENS

HOTEL CIPRIANI
Giudecca 10, 30133 Venice, Italy
Open Garden open to dining and hotel guests only
C + 39 041 520 7744
FAX + 39 041 520 3930
@ info@hotelcipriani.it
W www.hotelcipriani.com

SISSINGHURST
Cranbrook, Kent, England
Open Mar–Nov 11 am–6.30 pm
C + 44 (0) 15 8071 0701
W www.nationaltrust.org.uk/Sissinghurst

LA FOCE
61, Strada della Vittoria, Chianciano Terme, Italy
Open Guided tours Wed every hour 3–7 pm
(April–Sept) and 3–5 pm (Oct–Mar)
C FAX + 39 057 869 101
@ info@lafoce.com
W www.lafoce.com

CLIPPED PERFECTION

RYŌAN-JI
C +81 75 463 2216
Gardens nearby include the Gold Pavilion and
Ninna-ji.
Go to the Japan Tourist Office in your city for maps
and opening times.

LEVENS HALL
Kendal, Cumbria LA8 OPD, England
Open Mar–Oct, Sun–Thur 10 am–5 pm (house
12–4.30 pm)
☎ + 44 15 3956 0321
FAX + 44 15 3956 0669
@ houseopening@levenshall.co.uk
W www.levenshall.co.uk

BROUGHTON CASTLE
Broughton, near Banbury, Oxfordshire
OX15 5EB, England
Open Spring and summer
☎ FAX + 44 12 9527 6070
@ info@broughtoncastle.co
W www.broughtoncastle.com

GREAT FOSTERS
Stroude Rd, Egham, Surrey TW20 9UR, England
Open Garden open to dining and hotel guests only
☎ + 44 17 8443 3822
FAX + 44 17 8447 2455
@ enquiries@greatfosters.co.uk
W www.greatfosters.co.uk

COLLECTORS' GARDENS

ISOLA BELLA AND ISOLA MADRE
Via Stresa, Lake Maggiore, Italy
Open Mid Mar – mid Oct, daily 9 am–5 pm
www.borromeoturismo.it
For more information on Lake Maggiore and
its islands, villages and restaurants:
www.distrettolaghi.it

NEWBY HALL
Ripon, North Yorkshire HG4 5AE, England
Open Late Mar – late Sept, 11 am–5 pm
(house opens 12 pm)
☎ + 44 0845 450 4068
W www.newbyhall.co.uk

ROWALLANE
Saintfield, Balynahinch, County Down
(near Belfast), Ireland
Open Daily, except some public holidays,
10 am–4 pm
☎ + 44 28 9751 0131
W www.nationaltrust.org.uk/
main/w-rowallanegarden

SINGAPORE BOTANIC GARDENS
1 Cluny Rd, Singapore
Open Daily, 5 am–midnight; National Orchid
Garden 8.30 am–7.30 pm (entrance fees apply)
W www.sbg.org.sg or www.nparks.gov.sg

NOOROO
11–15 Church Lane, Mount Wilson, NSW 2786,
Australia
Open First weekend in Sept – last in Nov
☎ + 61 (0) 2 4756 2018 or + 61 (0) 2 9628 8411

ARTISTS' GARDENS

WOODBRIDGE
North Island, New Zealand
Open All year by appointment
☎ FAX + 64 9415 7525
@ www.woodbridgegardens@xtra.co.nz
W www.newzealand.com

LA MORTELLA
Via F Calise, 39 80075 Forio, Ischia (Na), Italy
Open April–Oct Tues, Thur, Sat and Sun 9 am–7 pm
@ info@lamortella.org
W www.lamortella.it/ for musical events

LA CASELLA
23 Chemins de Moulin, 06650 Opio le Rouret,
Alpes Maritime, France
Open Groups strictly by appointment
Write to Mr Claus Scheinhert at La Casella

For the sculptor Bronwyn Berman
☎ + 61 (0) 414318228
@ bronwyn.berman@pol.net.au

BEBEAH
The Avenue, Mount Wilson, NSW 2786, Australia
Open Groups by appointment
☎ FAX + 61 (0) 2 4756 2014

GRAND PASSIONS

MOUNT STEWART
Portaferry Rd, Newtownards, County Down
BT22 2AD, Ireland
Open Mar–Oct, 10 am–4 pm (later in spring,
summer and autumn)
W www.nationaltrust.org.uk or www.tourismireland
.com.au

ILNACULLIN
Garinish Island, Glengarriff, Ireland
Take small ferry from Glengarriff
Open Daily beginning Mar – end Oct

COTON MANOR
Coton, Guilsborough, Northamptonshire
NN6 8 RQ, England
Open Late Mar – late Sept, Tues–Sat, bank holidays
weekends and Sun in April and May, 12 noon–5.30 pm
Garden lectures.
☎ + 44 (0) 16 0474 0219
FAX + 44 (0) 16 0474 0838
@ pasleytyler@cotonmanor.co.uk
W www.cotonmanor.co.uk

YARRAWA
Open By appointment.
Write to: the owner, Burrawang, NSW 2577,
Australia

LARNACH CASTLE
145 Camp Rd, Otago Peninsula, Dunedin,
New Zealand
Open Daily 9 am–5 pm
☎ + 64 3476 1616
FAX + 64 3476 1574
@ larnach@larnachcastle.co.nz
W www.larnachcastle.co.nz

LISMORE CASTLE

Lismore, County Waterford, Ireland

Open Daily mid Mar – end Sept, 11 am–4.45 pm

C + 35 3585 4424

@ lismoreestates@eircom.net

W www.lismorecastle.com

HOLKER HALL

Cark-in-Cartmel, nr Grange-over-Sands, Cumbria
LA11 7PL, England

Open Gardens daily except Sat,
mid Mar – early Nov 10.30 am–5.30 pm

C + 44 (0) 15 3955 8328

FAX + 44 (0) 15 3955 8378

@ info@holker.co.uk

W www.holker-hall.co.uk

MONA

Little River Rd, Braidwood, NSW 2622, Australia

Open Garden open to dining and hotel guests only

C FAX + 61 (0) 2 4842 1288

@ schneider@mona.com.au

W www.weddings-nsw.com.au or www.mona.com.au
There is also accommodation in the historic coach
house and converted stables.

NINNA-JI

33 Ouchi Omuru Ukuo-ku, Kyoto, Japan

Open 9 am–4.30 pm

SAIHO-JI

56 Kamigaya-cho, Matsuo, Nishikyo-ku, Kyoto, Japan
Several weeks ahead of your visit, write with name,
address in Japan, occupation, age (you must be over
18), number of people and preferred (and alternative)
date(s) you wish to visit. Include self-addressed
envelope (stamped or with international reply
coupons) and mail to the address above (if you are
already in Japan, you should send a double postcard or *o-fuku hagaki*). Arrive five minutes early.

ALLERTON GARDENS

Southshore Kauai (near Poipu), Hawaii, USA
Reservations required.

C + 1 (808) 742 2623

W www.ntbg.org
Poipu Bay Golf: www.poipubaygolf.com
Princeville Golf: www.princeville.com

Atlee, Helena, *Italian Gardens*, Frances Lincoln, London, 2006.

Banks, David P & Perkins, Andrew, *Flora's Orchids*, ABC Books, Sydney, 2005.

Beales, P, *Classic Roses*, HarperCollins, London, 1997.

Bennett, Jennifer, *Lilacs for the Garden*, Firefly Books, Ontario, 2002.

Bisgrove, Richard, *The English Garden*, Viking, London, 1990

Bliss, Mildred, *Beatrix Jones Farrand: An Appreciation of a Great Gardener*, Judd & Detweiler, Washington, 1960.

Brooker, MIH & Kleinig, DA, *Field Guide to Eucalypts*, vol. 1, Blooming Books, Melbourne, 1999.

Brown, Jane, *Sissinghurst: Portrait of a Garden*, Weidenfeld & Nicolson, London, 1990.

Campbell-Culver, Maggie, *The Origin of Plants*, Headline, London, 2001.

Cave, Yvonne, *Succulents for the Contemporary Garden*, Florilegium, Sydney, 2002.

Clebsch, Betsy, *The New Book of Salvias*, Florilegium, Sydney, 2003.

Crowe, Sylvia, *Tomorrow's Landscape*, The Architectural Press, London, 1956.

Dirr, AS & Michael, A, *Hydrangeas for American Gardens*, Timber Press, Portland, 2004.

Earle, Joe, *Infinite Spaces: The Art and Wisdom of the Japanese Garden*, Tuttle Publishing, Tokyo, 2000.

Editors of *The Golf Insider*, *Golf Travel by Design*, The Globe Pequot Press, Connecticut, 2003.

Etherington, Kate, *Flora's Trees and Shrubs*, ABC Books, Sydney, 2005.

Farrand, Beatrix, *The Bulletins of Reef Point Gardens*, The Island Foundation, New York, 1997.

Gardiner, Jim, *Magnolias: A Gardener's Guide*, Timber Press, Oregon, 2000.

Griswold, Mac, *Washington's Gardens at Mount Vernon: Landscape of the Inner Man*, Houghton, New York, 1999.

— & Weller, Eleanor, *The Golden Age of American Gardens, 1890–1940*, Harry N Abrams, New York, 1991.

Hillier Nurseries, *The Hillier Manual of Trees & Shrubs*, David & Charles, Devon, 1994.

Jefferson, Thomas, *Thomas Jefferson's Garden Book*, facsimile, 1944.

Jekyll, Gertrude, *Colour in the Flower Garden*, Mitchell Beazley, London, 1995 edn.

— *Lost Garden: The Restoration of an Edwardian Masterpiece*, Garden Art Press, Suffolk, 2000

— & Weaver, Lawrence, *Gardens for Small Country Houses*, Antique Collectors Club, Suffolk, 1981 edn.

Jellicoe, G, *Collected Works*, vol. 2, Woodbridge, Antique Collectors Club, 1995.

—, Goode, P & Lancaster, M, *The Oxford Companion to Gardens*, Oxford University Press, Oxford, 1991.

Jones, David L, *A Complete Guide to Native Orchids of Australia*, New Holland, Sydney, 2006.

Kelly, J (ed.), *Hillier Gardener's Guide to Trees and Shrubs*, David & Charles Devon, Devon, 1995.

Kerr Forsyth, Holly, *Remembered Gardens: Eight Women and Their Visions of an Australian Landscape*, Melbourne, Miegunyah Press, 2006.

— *The Constant Gardener: A Botanical Bible*, Miegunyah Press, Melbourne, 2007.

Kostial McGuire, Diane, *Beatrix Farrand's Plant Book for Dumbarton Oaks*, Washington, 1980.

— & Fern, Lee, *Beatrix Jones Farrand: Fifty Years of American Landscape Architecture*, Dumbarton Oaks Publishing Service, Washington, 1982.

Lee, Hermione, *Edith Wharton*, Vintage Books, London, 2008.

Masson, Georgina, *Rome*, 2nd edn, Woodbridge, Suffolk, 1976.

Mathew, Brian & Swindells, Philip, *The Complete Book of Bulbs*, Mitchell Beazley, Sydney, 1995.

Nakane, Kinsaku, *Kyoto Gardens*, 22nd edn, Hoikusha, Osaka, 1992.

Origo, Iris, *Images and Shadows*, John Murray, London, 1970.

Page, Russell, *The Education of a Gardener*, Penguin Books, London, 1962.

Phillips, Roger & Rix, Martyn, *Perennials*, vols 1–2, Macmillan, London, 1994.

Plumptre, George, *Garden Ornament: Five Hundred Years of History and Practice*, Thames & Hudson, London, 1989.

Pourjavady, Nasrollah (ed.), *The Splendour of Iran*, vols 1–3, Booth-Clibborn Editions, London, 2001.

Qingxi, Lou, *Chinese Gardens*, China Intercontinental Press, 2003.

Riffle, Robert Lee, *The Tropical Look: An Encyclopaedia of Landscape Plants*, Thames & Hudson, London, 1998.

Robinson, William, *Home Landscapes*, John Murray, London, 1914.

— *The English Flower Garden*, 8th edn, John Murray, London, 1900.

Rogers, Elizabeth Barlow, *Landscape Design: A Cultural and Architectural History*, Harry Abrams, New York, 2001.

Ross, Graham et al, *Botanica*, Random House, Sydney, 1997.

Russell, Vivian, *Edith Wharton's Italian Gardens*, Frances Lincoln, London, 1997.

Sackville-West, Vita, *Passenger to Tehran*, Arrow Books, London, 1991 edn.

Short, Philip, *In Pursuit of Plants*, University of Western Australia Press, Perth, 2003.

Stroud, Dorothy, *Capability Brown*, London Country Life Limited, London, 1984 edn.

Tachibana-no-Toshitsuna, *Sakuteiki (Notes on Garden Design)*, trans. Takei, Jiro & Keane, Marc P, Tuttle Publishing, Tokyo, 2001.

Tamulevich, Susan, *Dumbarton Oaks: Garden into Art*, Monacelli Press, New York, 2001.

Targuebayre, Claire, *Cordes en Abigeois*, privately published, Toulouse, 1988 edn.

Valder, Peter, *The Garden Plants of China*, Florilegium, Sydney, 1999.

— *Gardens in China*, Florilegium, Sydney, 2002.

Walton, Susana, *La Mortella: An Italian Garden Paradise*, New Holland, London, 2002.

Wharton, Edith, *Italian Villas and Their Gardens*, Century Company, New York, 1904, facsimile edition, Rizzoli, New York, 2008.

— & Codman, Ogden, Jr, *The Decoration of Houses*, WW Norton, New York, 1978 edn.

Wilson, Ernest, *China, Mother of Gardens*, Waterstone & Co., London, 1985.

— *Smoke that Thunders*, Waterstone, London, 1985 edn.

Young, David & Michiko, *The Art of the Japanese Garden*, Tuttle Publishing, Hong Kong, 2005.

THE MIEGUNYAH PRESS

This book was designed by Pfisterer + Freeman
The text was typeset by Pfisterer + Freeman
The text was set in 9½ point Archer
with 14 points of leading
The text is printed on 130 gsm matt art paper
This book was copyedited by Judy Brookes